Kith Review

ISSUE 1 | ABUNDANCE | AUTUMN, 2022

I0184935

CONTENTS

Kith Review is published by Cinnamon Press
Office 49019
PO Box 15113
Birmingham
B2 2NJ
info@cinnamonpress.com

cinnamonpress.com/kith-review/

Editor: Jan Fortune and Adam Craig
Design & Layout: Adam Craig

ISBN 978-1-78864-805-9

Submission details and subscription information:
cinnamonpress.com/kith-review/

Thank you to all those who pre-ordered the first issues of *Kith Review* and to those who sponsored the new venture.

Particular thanks to Mark Charlton and Richard Douglas Pennant, our founding sponsors. And to all the other generous sponsors:

John Barnie, Anne Bateman, Mick Evans, Suzanna Fitzpatrick, Evie Ford, Paula Greenwood, E A Griffiths, Dorothy Judd, Sue Kaberry, Sue Lewis, Isabelle Llasera, David Mills, Kelly Moffett, Diana Powell, Paula Read, Bonnie Thurston, Sarah Watkinson, Jeremy Worman and Teffy Wrightson.

Editorial

Jan Fortune

I come from a family that has endless stories of scarcity. My mother, from an Irish immigrant family of 11 children, repeated these stories endlessly—Christmas would bring an apple and orange and if the orange was eaten before lunch the child would be beaten; jam jars were used as cups; food was meagre and cheap; security and love were in even shorter supply in a home where violence was an ever-present threat and a commonplace reality. When I was a child I would often be woken by her screams as she relived her childhood in nightmares. She married above her family, moving from underclass to working class, but in the first years of the marriage my dad would have to walk the 6 miles to work for part of each week as there wasn't enough money to afford the bus fare for the whole week. They continued to struggle for many years, gradually finding some security before recession brought huge unemployment in Teesside, including for my dad. I carried the scarcity stories into my first marriage and at the end of it, after 31 years, was left with a house in negative equity and debts. The generations of scarcity stories and the mentality they encouraged in my family are not unusual—in rich countries the gap between the rich and the poor gets ever wider. In poorer countries scarcity is routinely life-threatening.

And yet we live on an abundant planet, despite humanity's efforts to pollute and degrade it. And at its core, abundance is not a measurement. In a world where there is such a sharp divide between living in riches or scarcity, and an increasingly complex media that encourages dissatisfaction and want, we often, and understandably, confuse abundance with consumption. There is nothing romantic about poverty. But abundance is not about having things, or acquiring more and more 'stuff'. It's about how we savour life, the ability to delight in the everyday pleasures that surround us. Abundance comes in those moments when we are truly alive to the present and in how we connect with all life.

I'm often taken by surprise at how much life can change with a simple shift of perspective. When we are viewing life from a sense of overwhelm, it's so easy to fall into the malaise of seeing everything in terms of what is lacking. We saw this in the UK during the first lockdown, with strange and unnecessary shortages of basic things: toilet roll, pasta, surface cleaners… People felt or feared, rather than experienced, that there was 'not enough' and the sense of lack became a self-fulfilling prophesy as people panicked and over-bought these commodities. A story of 'not enough' became an actual scarcity that never needed to be.

Stories are powerful, as I learnt from my family's tales of scarcity. They can keep us living small-minded, contracted lives. But the opposite is also true. Just being alive is an extraordinary miracle and when we start to delight in this then abundance becomes a way of living and an act of hope. It's the inverse of living from fear and takes the focus away from the small ego-centred self to enable us to be more outward-looking. Perhaps that's one of the reasons why so many stories of generosity centre on people who don't, in material terms, have a great deal and yet freely give.

And it is also a witness to the extent to which abundance is a powerful story that we can live by and change the world by. This inaugural issue of *Kith Review* is full of such stories—as essays, poems, prose, and narratives, as pictures, songs, scientific exploration, yoga nidrā and more… an abundance of reflections using the abundant wealth of language and imagery.

Making the perspective shift from scarcity to abundance is not a claim that we're already living in utopia or should only write about fluffy bunnies finding an eternal source of carrots. We won't get to utopia without telling some truths about the current bankrupt systems of power and abuse that prevail on our planet. Abundance isn't a perspective for those who want to hide in La-la Land. Rather, it's a mindset for those brave enough to find joy, hope and gratitude even in the midst of chaos, illness, loss, sorrow and mess. It's the language of those with enough vision to weave new stories even in desperate times.

The writers in this issue have this vision. Ultimately, abundance is about how we inhabit and make sense of the world, how we are at home (or not) in ourselves and connected to all of life. When we stop stressing about having more stuff or being on top or always having control; when we don't distract ourselves with food, shopping, drink, over-work… or whatever our particular poison is, then we stop living within the stories of scarcity and instead face ourselves with both honesty and kindness. We begin to live in abundance. It's never a final destination of course. Some days, the sense of scarcity comes flooding in. Some days the clay of our writing is clogged with clichés and refuses to be fashioned into anything fresh and true. But we know abundance is all around us and we can gently begin again, and again.

This issue is such a beginning—a beautiful one—and I hope you will delight in its abundance. KR

Fiona Owen

Three Summer Haibun

I Rowan

Noticing the rowan tree reach top tips upwards, maxing out on light as the earth tilts on its axis, solstice-time, making good to grow while it can, digging in deeper so as to take, from the sources of above and below, nourishment. There will be fire-berries, orange first then the red of our kitchen wall, that hang in heavy clusters that the birds feast on. Protector tree here as the summer starts and daylight peaks.

40th birthday
present, tree of life's journey
many dogs ago

II Making hay

As I sip coffee, I find myself glancing at a small clump of grasses that we've overlooked in the border where the fuchsia is. Now, they're tall and the breeze makes ballet dancers of them with their graceful bend and sway. Common old oat-grass loaded with seed-heads, it would be anonymous in the field; here, though, it's crept into view, as if to say 'we too deserve your gaze'. The tractor is cutting hay in the field just over the hedge from us. Grasses like this lie in lines to dry—it's perfect hay-making weather that's forecast for this week. Baled and barned, it will feed their horses over winter. This oat-grass behind the fuchsia droops with the weight of its fruit, spilling itself forward, the breeze helping it empty.

Used coffee cup
on the table, the window
an open eye

III Saint John's Wort

The hypericum bush is covered in waxy yellow stars, the flowers that are said to bloom around John the Baptist's birthday, the 24th June. This year, they're a little late, but what's a couple of weeks in the life of a summer? Our garden is full of memories: trees or shrubs carrying something of the person who gifted them. Olive, rowan, mahonia, sweet chestnut—so many interconnections. I think of who gave us the St John's Wort, so many years ago, when she was still speaking to us. The flowers carry a story of healing, but not everyone knows how to soften what's stony within them. People lose their heads—and John did, literally, though he was healer, baptiser, prophet. Life's vagaries. I don't hold anything against this beautiful shrub, so well grown and healthy, thriving in its place by the rowan tree. It was a small bush when given, and now look at it.

Paracelsus knew
even in those early times—
flowerherb heartlift KR

Stephanie Percival

coming back to the world
is a slow process

Songs for Recovery

Day 1

Kraaaw!

Kraaaw, Kraaaw… Crow's squawking alarm cuts deep into my sluggish brain. I pull the sheets back over my head. Sink back into dreams of darkness.

Day 2

One long piping call… then another even sweeter. I open an eye, stiff, encrusted with salt. Silt left from tears.

Re… peat… Re… peat… I obey the thrush's call. Open both eyes. Squint at the day.

Sound slips between the curtains as filaments of light, trembling in the smog of the room.

There's a chair draped with crumpled clothes. A glass at the bedside, still water beaded with stale bubbles.

Day 3

A melody plays. Strung and hung from the branches of the cherry tree outside. My feet stumble as I move to the window. An aura of tainted air clings to me, acid breath and body sweat.

Blackbird sits silhouetted, its yellow beak a beacon behind broderie anglaise blossom.

Dawn sun breaches the horizon; the sky is distant… breaks through in blue.

Day 4

Robin chirrups outside the kitchen window… busy… busy, scrutinises me as I put the kettle on the hob. He chides me with a twiddle dee… twiddle doo… why are you standing there… things to be done.

I watch his sharp flight, crisscrossing the garden, marking his boundary.

The kettle whistles as it boils. Water singing as I pour it in the cup.

Day 5

Come on… come on… come on… great tit greets me as I step onto the path. The ground cold and rough beneath bare feet.

The cottage garden is overgrown. Left unattended too long. Now laden with blossom. Floral perfume saturates the air, damp against my skin. Grainy grasses brush against my legs as I weave along the path, scattering seed patterns on my pyjamas.

Come on… come on… great tit encourages. But I can go no further.

Day 6

The tea cup on the tray rattles as I walk to the end of the garden.

The gazebo is draped with ivy making a dark cave. The wooden chair is damp but I sit and peep out. My heart beats a solemn pulse, echoing within the green space.

Light over the garden is grey, muting flowers to a wash of pink, violet and pewter. I sip my tea, hot and sweet on my tongue.

Warbling burbles from the greenery. The small specked brownness of a wren squats in the shadow matrix of entangled branches.

I imagine it trembling with effort. Its lungs miniature bellows, expending all breath to sing.

Day 7—Dawn Chorus

The garden is different today. An abundance of bird song, morning scent, light and shade. It overloads my senses. The smell is greenness rubbed against skin, like dock leaves.

I sit and watch splashes of sunlight spill through branches, dappling me with healing balm.

The daily orchestra warms up, violins and pipes and whistles. Woodpecker drums in the distance and timpani of sparrows chatter-chitter from hedgerows. Pigeons add harmony in rhythmic coo… coo… coos. My steady breathing augments the chorus.

I make plans, to mow the grass, weed the borders… feed the roses.

Nothing needs to be done quickly.

The birds will still sing their songs tomorrow.

Bonnie Thurston

Christmas 2020

'…resting against the naked breast of life…' — *Etty Hillesum*

As I do, the little birds
tough out winter here
in frozen hills enfolding
the Ohio River valley,
today puff up like oranges
that were always tucked
way down in the tippy toes
of our Christmas stockings.

This frigid, festal morning
on two sides of the feeder
a bright, crimson Cardinal,
an ordinary brown sparrow
pick toward the corner.
They will meet, nibbling
their unearned, freely given
Christmas breakfast.

Both are cold and hungry, but
neither drives the other away
from wizened, stippled seeds
that once were summer's
glorious, golden Sunflowers,
now being transformed
into a feathered fluttering
that presses bravely toward life.

Sunday Morning

I do not put on
a fancy dress with
elaborate matching hat,
but something simple.
Before leaving
for 8 a.m. Eucharist,
I watch a male Cardinal
feed his mate seeds.

Fog still hangs in our
little valley, but disperses
as I carefully drive
up the serpentine road
to the parish church
with a glorious view
of the surrounding hills.

Hoping sight always
clears as we ascend,
I delight to see that,
this summer morning,
every blade of grass,
no matter how mere,
wears a perfect pearl
of no price at all.

Promissory

In the background
the skeletal pattern
of winter weary trees
yearns for first
leaves to explode
in yellow-green puffs.
In the foreground,
the vivid, deep purple
of old lilacs droop
cones of blossom from
heart shaped leaves
as summer's first bees
busy themselves
in sweetness
I see with my nose,
and with my ears
hear the buzz that
promises honey. KR

Simon Jackson

Tadpoles

Again I've been scooping up the stuff of life.
A jam jar rubs against my groin,
filled, hopefully, with swarming tadpoles
too tiny for the eye to see,
keeping the sample body temp
as I cycle to the clinic.

Awaiting is not a bowl in my window
but Petri dish and pipette.

Across the years my eight-year old self
cycles excitedly beside me,
impatient for his jar of slippery spawn
to mutate into writhing life.

Geography

Seismic forces have upturned the topography
of your body and I'm left without the tools
or means to map or measure them.
The undulating desert sands of stomach,
the shallow dunes of breasts are unrecognisable.

No storm has thrown these new contours,
no ice-age calving fresh arêtes,
peaks and troughs, alluvial ridges,
nor ocean waves sculpting vast cliffs.

Your new form is perfect, not forced by fault-lines'
friction, the heat of new life bubbling
is the furnace that forges this mountain,
smooth and warm as fresh-blown glass,
miraculous as a new-formed star.

Three Ages

Lying curled against your mother's belly
you are a fairground mirror's image,
mother to daughter; each one
an undulating sea of smooth curves.

Daughter facing son, face to face,
unaware of the other's existence,
one out, one still within
a before and after shot

or a cut away section
in a medical textbook;
mother and child and child to be
a vision of past, present and future,

Klimpt's three ages painted in
the afternoon sun's gold,
the window's shadow framing and patterning
what was, is, and what will be

and I am overwhelmed by such love for the three of you,
I am shocked to sudden tears
and leave the room blinking them back
before you get concerned and ask me

what is wrong?
and I'm forced to admit
that for once, there is nothing;
everything is absolutely, perfectly right.

Anne Bateman

The Field

the view is boundless green
        -garden to field to wall of oak

where keening red kites nest
and other animal calls sound

        deer and boar, hunted in autumn,
race and bleed on barbed wire,

so when the farmer steps back,
leaving the earth to reknit,

it breathes each blade's push to
catch light, a refracting

waist-high churning, a summer pelt
of silk sliding on wind.

No more rivers of black slugs
fleeing a chemical dissolution,

but a border of buttercups,
flanking barbed wire,

and as the dawn dew draws down
grass heads, heavy with drenching

each stem threads an arc of droplets,
multiple moons—crescents of reflected sky

From dust to dirt

however much we toil
there is no end
only this ever present
raising dust
sweeping reeds across the floor,
bare feet rootling in smooth earth
damp cloths reveal matter made new
brass buffed to an untarnished shine
—hedging time

while outside in all
that tended symmetry
a rush of dandelions
their double-headed suns
in a mandala of bitter leaves,
roots tapping deep
flowers chasing light in a karaoke blaze,
rejected for the posies
turn to fragile geometry
and empty on a breath

Roquiague

It's been a slow
gathering roll, these undulating hills
I couldn't see at first
a lag
like looking at postcards
beautiful but my heart was cold

I pined for the familiar
          bluebells and brambles
but, with no escape,
we huddled round the fire
for the winter

Arrokiaga, place of rock,
a spring seeping through
the mountain's cracked foot
where once
the secret walls of oak
came down to the river bank,
hunters tracked deer
 drawn here to drink,
or tickled trout
in shimmer-heat of summer
shelter—exchanged news, pelts,
followed the river's slow gradient
to the higher mountains.

Now, the same rushy river
flooding or shallow-scraping bedrock.
I hear a high tin whistle
breaking the silence of the valley,
see feet dance
in patterns, delicate as lace—
circle hand in hand,
bodies weaving
infinity—warp and weft

We venture out as
days lengthen
recognising the shapes of the mountains
—Pic d'Ani, Ayus

Held in the meltwater of their rivers,
walking through heavy dew
uncurling in the warm salt water
seeping from the rock
kites circling above,

our solitary totemic guardian
a grubby heron
surprised into disjointed take off
lifts, dragging gravity,
unfurling her unwieldy wings
circles the valley
flapping over
stone crafted houses,
the cleared land,
the tended beasts,
the same names. KR

1
61
2
14
3
26
13
60
27
28
29
30
31
59
4

Generous Abundance

UMA DINSMORE TULI

A celebratory pilgrimage through the realms of Nidrā Shakti Queen of Rest and Dreams... and all the places in between

At a time when the only radical act remaining may be to *rest*, I welcome you here, dear one. Please know, you are so warmly welcome. Just as you are. I invite you here to become once more your fully rested self; to be nourished by the generous abundance of the yoga of sleep. I welcome you into a restful meditation in the timeless land of surrender to sleep.

Can you let yourself be nowhere and everywhere at once? This is a spacious place that you can call your own... the space simply to be lucidly conscious of becoming unconscious.

Let me be your guide now as we travel together through these pathless lands of lucid sleep. Ours is a sacred journey in prose and praise, and verse and song, and all the places in between. The language may be foreign, but the welcome is felt deep, in tired bones that long to rest and settle into sleep, to carry us to threshold places we already know. But just before you drop right off, can you notice this? This generous magic of the in-between?

अनागतायां नद्रिायां प्रणष्टे बाह्य गोचरे।
सावस्था मनसा गमया पर देवी प्रकशते॥

anāgatāyāṁ nidrāyāṁ praṇaṣṭe bāhya gocare |
sāvasthā manasā gamayā para devī prakaśate ||

Before deep sleep has settled in to steal away alert recall,
Between this sleep and waking state, whilst outer world recedes from sense,
Then our perception, turned within, becomes aware of consciousness;
And at that moment, resting mind perceives the space between the states
To be the place where She reveals her supreme nature as She is:
The energy of consciousness.

(*Vijñāna Bhairava Tantra*, v.75)

This place is Yoga Nidrā's space... here is where she rules. She is Yoga Nidrā Shakti Devī, the goddess of this liminal magic place, the threshold between waking and sleeping, between dreaming and rest... This is her home, she welcomes us home to our rested selves.

And who is she when she's at home? Let me share with you.

She has so many names... Her Sanskrit name is Yoga Nidrā Shakti. Sometimes called Devī too. Śri Yoga Nidrā Shakti Devī Mā is for best formal use (or just to be on the safe side). You may have heard of her.

But even if you do not know her many proper names, you will have met her. For every night she comes to find you. She comes to love you just as you are. I wonder can you still sense her? Can you feel her presence at the ragged edges of your dreams? She is the Wild Realm of Liminality. She is Nidrā Shakti, Queen of Sleep and Dreams. We meet her as she embraces us into the sleep state. She is encountered, amongst other places, in profound rest, and in those liminal states of consciousness experienced in the meditative practices of yoga nidrā, or the Sleep of the Yogis. She is the dark feminine power of sleep herself. With generosity, and an abundance of ways to help us drop off, with great kindness and an ever-expanding lap—She doesn't mind how we get to Her. She doesn't mind how we fall asleep. No-one can resist Her. She gets everybody in the end, no matter how much coffee we drink.

For indeed Yoga Nidrā Shakti is a generous and commanding South Asian goddess of sleep, rest, and liminal spaces between dreaming and waking. A key figure in The Great Victory of the goddess (Devī Mahātmyam, c600 BC), her Sanskrit name literally means the 'power of sleep'. A divine manifestation of the dark goddess of time herself—Kali—Nidrā Shakti features in many images and indigenous storytelling rituals, all celebrating Her power to send every being (including gods) to sleep. She wields the deep and generous power to welcome all beings to sleep. For wherever she appears, Nidrā Shakti is a divine bringer of rest: she counters the transgressions of those who refuse to sleep, returning humans (and gods) to right relationship with natural cycles. She nourishes abundant creativity, and her inspirational realms are lush with wild gardens of dream.

And here, right now, through images and words, this restful pilgrimage of pages celebrates the abundance of all healing and creativity gifted to humans by Nidrā Shakti.

1 Preparations for the pilgrimage...

Dear pilgrim now, go gentle. Let us move with respect and awe through the lands of Nidrā Shakti, for she has endless power. She has even brought Lord Vishnu, sustainer of creation in the Indic pantheon, under her sway. He snored sweetly in her power for over three thousand years, and no one could wake him, even when a pair of demons crawled from his earwax and threatened to devour Brahma, the Creator, who was resting in a lotus that had grown from the snoring Vishnu's navel. Yes indeed, she wields great power, and she has spread it widely.

Yogis, healers, indigenous shaman, poets, inventors, psychologists, stage hypnotists, medicine people and other fellow seekers after peace, Nidrā Shakti has travelled and slept with them all. In the fourteenth century she enjoyed the wild

sweet embraces of naked Kashmiri poet songstress Lalleshwari, as she sang of the interdependence of sleeping, waking and wisdom. Amongst her most admired liberatory adventures, she assisted the reparation and restoration of the Black Panther warrior kings of the mythic African nation of Wakanda. At other times in other places (often all at once) Nidrā Shakti inspired the rhapsodic visions of the Irish Nobel Laureate William Butler Yeats in London in 1888, and the composers of the Vijnana Bhairava Tantra in eleventh century India. She has danced through charmed encounters with Transcendentalists and Relaxationists in 19th century Massachusetts. Her intimates include Lal Ded, Octavia Butler, Twylah Nitsch, Henry David Thoreau, Annie Payson Call, William Butler Yeats, Thomas Edison, Leonardo DaVinci, Salvador Dalí, and a crew of yogic gurus with ambiguous reputations, such as Swami Satyananda Saraswati, Swami Rama and Amrit Desai, as well as a number of curious psychologists, and her greatest North American admirer, Ormond McGill, father of US stage hypnotism.

And Nidrā Shakti's relatives are numberless. Amongst her global kith and kin are the dream goddesses, the guardians, the ones who mind our rest. Nidrā Shakti's relatives and friends shine in the constellations of those entities who guard our nights, including the Bön Tibetan goddess of lucid sleep, Salgye du Dalma, and Nritti, the Vedic goddess of darkness and chaos. The sweetly generous Swapneshvari, goddess of lucid dream, is a cousin of hers, and across the continents, from Africa to America and from the mythic reaches of Norse and Celtic lands to the deep and ancient Dreamtime of the first peoples of Australasia, wisdom holders everywhere honour the magical multiplicity of threshold spaces at the hypnopompic boundaries of sleep and dream. These are her realms.

Having named Shri Nidrā Shakti and honoured the global constellation of her family and influence, we have learnt a little of her power. We can now begin our pilgrim travels through her realms of stillness together. Are you resting comfortably? Then I'll begin.

With a pause.

For the journey into sleep is not a linear path. It circles round and back again. Resting under her influence, we snooze, then stir and surface, and afterwards dive deep. And so too, this our pilgrimage is punctuated by pauses to give praise. Pauses to honour, as we travel through her lands, the abundant and generous Nidrā Shakti in each of the places we encounter her.

These pausing praises sing of one hundred and eight powers of the forms of Nidrā Shakti, the manifestation of the Power of Sleep. Here begins the naming of the ways She nurtures human lives through all times and in all worlds:

1 She who gives us rest—I honour Her.
2 She who eases our pain—I honour Her.
3 She who comforts us in our suffering—I honour Her.
4 She who heals our wounds—I honour Her.
5 She who cradles our grief—I honour Her.
6 She who remedies all ills—I honour Her.
7 She who quietens crying children—I honour Her.
8 She who relieves us from anxieties—I honour Her.
9 She who disentangles us from the knots of worry—I honour Her.
10 She who rescues the exhausted from the grind of work—
I honour Her.
11 She who relieves the befuddled from the pressures of thought—
I honour Her.
12 She who weaves the threads of memories into the fabric of now—
I honour Her.

I voice these praises so that we may know her generous nature.
Let me introduce myself, so you may know your guide, and settle into our journey together.

2 Settling in...

Rest as we travel the ragged edges of conscious awareness. Navigating our many ways through places of freedom and interdependence, I offer you safe passage through the fecund borderlands between states of sleep and waking. I've been here since 1969, when I first met Nidrā Shakti under my bed in North London, so I know my way around. Since I was four years old, I have been a hypnopompic servant of sleep. Fifty years on, this snoozer is become a well-dreamt biographer of the power of sleep herself, sharing what I have learnt from my travels in the pathless lands of Her realms.

For the past seven timeless years I've been a fractal encyclopaedist, writing the impossible biography of Nidrā Shakti—the Queen of Sleep and Dreams herself. Respectfully tracking and sharing the limitless abundance of the states of yoga nidrā, this project to honour her names and realms spirals through practice, devotions, and research. She is so vast that her biography has become a rare species of encyclopaedia, a compilation of stories, scientific experiments and sacred songs, a spectrum of memories, histories, healings, and homunculi.

Seven hundred and seventy pages are the gathering place of all I could find of her: physiology and psychology, esoterica, and quotidian miracles. Nidrā Shakti is everywhere, and she has assisted humans in countless ways for thousands of years. Healing from lightning injuries and hysterectomies, recovering after brain haemorrhages, or learning to freedive, humans have been helped in their sufferings and struggles by Nidrā Shakti.

Serving her story, writing her life, I have followed Nidrā Shakti into fractal echoes of trances shared together in twenty-seven different countries and states across this increasingly sleepless world of tired humans, all desperate to rest. On my global pilgrimage to all the places I can find her, I have served Nidrā Shakti by singing exhausted beings into the restful spaces between places, and soothing insomniacs into deep sleep by calling praises of the Queen of Sleep and Dream herself.

By this seventh year of writing the Encyclopaedia of Yoga Nidrā, I have encountered thirteen different named methods and forms of yoga nidrā. There are traditional schools of yoga in North India that deliver structured and prescriptive methods to access yoga nidrā through bossy injunctions not to fall asleep, scaring resters rigid as they try to relax; there are resolutely secular Californian methods developed by clinical psychologists, Turkish approaches from self-proclaimed masters that promise enlightenment, and stripped-down, highly efficient German micro-nidrās shared online for research purposes. There are lush Francophone varieties tested in Provence, Tamil species under investigation by graduate students in South Indian Ayruvedic Universities, and all manner of yoga nidrā in practice from Florida to Anatolia, and from Karnataka to Uttar Pradesh. Amidst this yogic abundance, across all her many forms, all of

them are simply different names and methods to arrive at similar encounters with Nidrā Shakti herself. For she is the power of Sleep, the active ingredient of all forms of yoga nidrā.

Some of those who profit from her power have trademarked their methods, and given her their own names, which can make it seem as if these new forms have nothing to do with Her Vast and Magnificent Abundantness, Śri Yoga Nidrā Shakti Devī Mā. But take it from her devoted biographer, all these forms are her alright. No matter how they call her, it's all her. Believe me, it all comes from the same place. Amongst so many names and forms, we recognise her by her abundant gifts:

13 She who knits up the ravelled sleave of care—I honour Her
14 She who clears paths in the garden of dreams—I honour Her.
15 She who spins the web of nightmare—I honour Her.
16 She who is the source of all inspiration—I honour Her.
17 She who is the fount of all song—I honour Her.
18 She who is the depths of the oceans of stories—I honour Her.
19 She who is the sanctuary of the oppressed—I honour Her.
20 She who is the crucible of revolution—I honour Her.
21 She who is the strengthener of resolve—I honour Her.
22 She who restores—I honour Her.
23 She who re-sets—I honour Her.
24 She who revives—I honour Her.

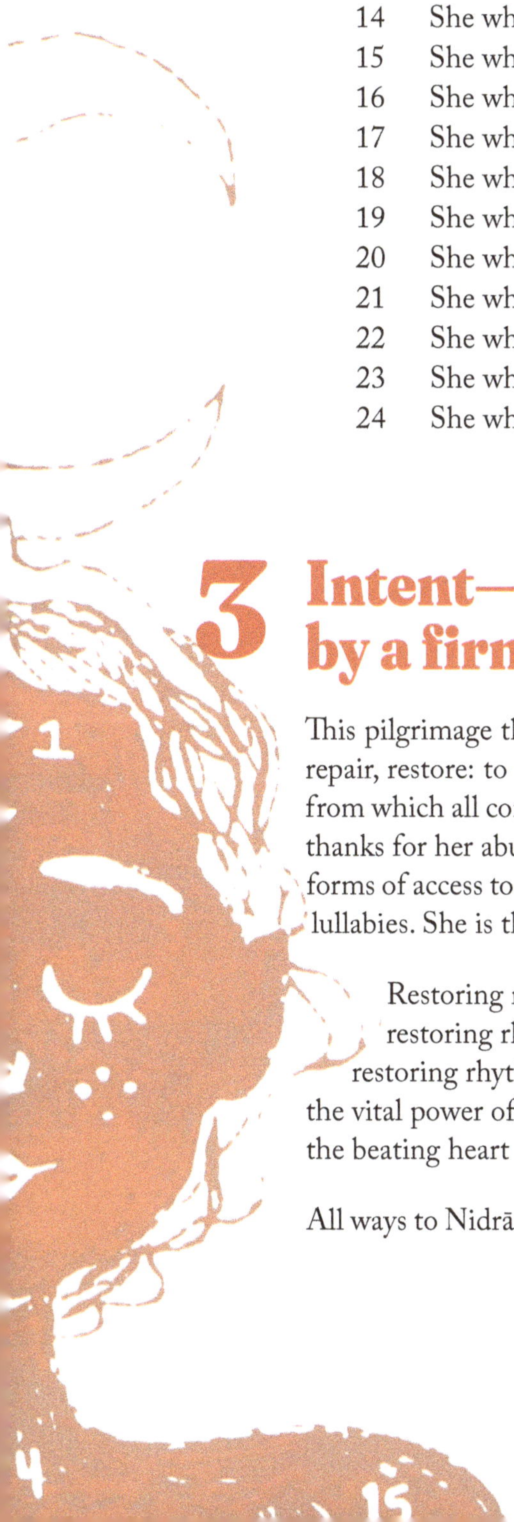

3 Intent—our pilgrim journey guided by a firm resolve...

This pilgrimage through Nidrā Shakti's realms cherishes a resolution to return, repair, restore: to give the generous gifts all back to her. For she is the essence from which all commodified and trademarked forms have been extracted. I offer thanks for her abundance and give her this land back. I note that all the ancient forms of access to her state are metrical—and rhythmical, in rhyme and metre—lullabies. She is the mother of our sleep who sings us into rest.

Restoring rhythmic cycles in the body of the earth,
restoring rhythmic cycles in this resting body now,
restoring rhythmic cycles in the place of restful being,
the vital power of body's cells is dancing to this pulse,
the beating heart of all that lives upon the body of this earth

All ways to Nidrā Shakti's realms rest on this rhythmic pulse, the pulse of life we share in verse. I give her this land back. Decolonise, indigenise and honour all these roots—so all can rest in naked ease, abundant and beloved. On cusping sleep, we reconnect with interbeing here.

25 She who nourishes—I honour Her.
26 She who nurtures—I honour Her.
27 She who empowers—I honour Her.
28 She who grants us freedom—I honour Her.
29 She who offers joy—I honour Her.
30 She who retrieves memory—I honour Her.
31 She who clarifies understanding—I honour Her.
32 She who gifts the wisdom of forgetting—I honour Her.
33 She who brings peace—I honour Her.
34 She who terrifies—I honour Her.
35 She who grants lucidity in dream and life—I honour Her.
36 She who reveals the truth—I honour Her.

4 Journeying through the places of deep rest to find healing...

And as we travel through her fecund liminal lands, this is where healing thrives. Those whose pain was lessened, those whose sight returned, those who broke when lightning struck, are all restored by her. The illnesses and sufferings, insomnia, and grief—recovery from surgery, relief of body's aches, the chorus of these testimonies is astonishing. And each individual song voices the same clear notes. It's so simple. When we rest, we make the space to heal. So menstrual cramps, and painful joints, headaches, and nausea too, are eased by resting in her realm. She helps us to feel well. She also wakes us up to truth: that tired bodies hurt the most, and our immunity is weakened when we skimp on sleep.

When I called out for testimonies to the healing power of yoga nidrā, waves of grateful praise flooded my inbox. People all over the world wrote to tell me how they'd listened to yoga nidrā during their chemotherapy sessions, or to prepare for and heal from major surgery. They spoke of how Nidrā Shakti held them through the labour of childbirth, or the depths of postnatal depression; they wrote of how yoga nidrā was at the core of their recovery from addictions and anxiety. Life after life was restored to brightness and abundance through the simple processes of resting in the arms of Yoga Nidrā Shakti...

there is wisdom in forgetting
there is healing in this sleep
there is dropping out of worry when we finally let go

when we let go of our holding on to stay in wakefulness—

37 She who lets us die to delusion—I honour Her.
38 She who shows us love is more powerful than reason—
I honour Her.
39 She who liberates the enslaved—I honour Her.
40 She who unlocks the imprisoned—I honour Her.
41 She who frees us from our bodies—I honour Her.
42 She who frees us from our minds—I honour Her.
43 She who holds heavy and light together at the same time—
I honour Her.
44 She who feeds the soul—I honour Her.
45 She who shows us death—I honour Her.
46 She who boosts the production of breastmilk—I honour Her.
47 She who is the pause between contractions in childbirth—
I honour Her.
48 She who makes babies and children grow—I honour Her.

5 A playful time with paradox

And in the very midst of the labyrinth of our journey with her, deep in the heart of all abundance, we notice something strange. After we have travelled our awareness around our resting body we arrive here. At a pair of opposites. We may notice that we are aware—whilst resting in lucid sleep. We taste the waking dream of full awareness while we rest.

And here's another paradox—dear pilgrim, can you sense? Can you perceive this paradox? The many seeking to make one. For there is a world of diligent researchers focussed on one aim—to explain the multiplicity of just how the yoga nidrā states are felt, and what occurs in this place of simply being.

The researchers ask: how can this be named, used, and applied? Since 1970 here have been 84 experiments to try to pin her down, 30 books and hundreds of researchers' diligent efforts to dissect her, observe and count and chart yoga nidrā. This is the way they strive to own and take apart all that she is. And still she thrives to generate abundance.

Even in the laboratories, the healing that she brings is a world of nourishment—the nurture seeping in. She is so vast she cannot be contained and codified. Let us forage in the fertile forests of yoga nidrā studies, research papers and investigations—what shall we find? There are meta-analyses by Korean researchers, and technical evaluations in Oregon, detailing multiple psychometric and biometric data to indicate the nature of the yoga nidrā experience. Studies, case studies, literature reviews and clinicians' evaluations all tell of the multiplicity of ways that yoga nidrā is experienced.

Back in the 1970s and 90s, researchers began simply by asking, what is happening inside people's brains during yoga nidrā? They recruited expert practitioners and scanned their brains in Topeka, Kansas, Copenhagen and London, and found, amongst other things, that brainwave states and other apparently autonomous functions of the nervous systems, including levels of endogenous neurotransmitters such as dopamine, could be consciously controlled through the practice of yoga nidrā. As a result of these findings, the focus of most research into yoga nidrā during the first decade of this century was upon how the practice could be used to relieve stress.

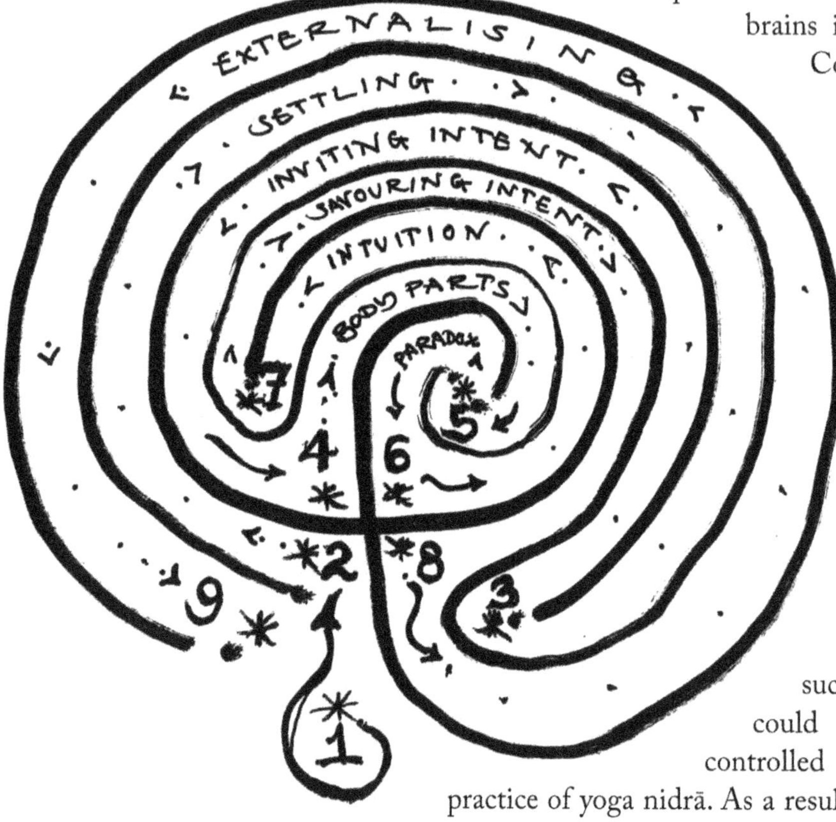

But then the vast fertile realms of Nidrā Shakti began to bear fruit and the diversity of research exploded… Since 2016 there have been over eighty-four studies in eleven different countries. A few are still focused on identifying what happens neurologically in yoga nidrā, but most of this new wave of studies explore how yoga nidrā can be applied to relieve suffering. What kind of suffering? All kinds. Dear pilgrim, let me introduce you to seven kinds of suffering that span the globe of yoga nidrā research.

In a clinic in Wuhan, fifty elderly people in need of colonoscopies were fortunate enough to be part of the yoga nidrā experimental group to discover if practising yoga nidrā whilst having a small camera inserted through your anus was more, or less painful than experiencing the same procedure whilst listening to a special relaxing medley of Mozart piano concertos. It was. And the colonoscopist reported it was easier to insert the camera in the pensioners who were listening to a yoga nidrā track than the ones listening to Mozart. On a post-partum recovery ward in Southern Thailand, 124 postnatal women listened to yoga nidrā recordings within two hours of giving birth, so that the researchers could discover if yoga nidrā would lessen post-partum fatigue and support postnatal recovery—it did. The leader of the experiment was so impressed, she wrote an article about it in The Journal of Thai Nursing Practice, calling for every woman to listen to yoga nidrā after birth. In Oregon, a research team set up a sleep lab protocol to discover if all the people who said that yoga nidrā helped them to go to sleep were right—they discovered that they were, for indeed, under laboratory conditions they could evaluate all the psychometric and biometric indicators of a shortened latent sleep onset period. School children with ADHD in Sydney who practised yoga nidrā were found to have less behavioural problems; women in Lucknow with severe menstrual disorders had their symptoms relieved; and the stress levels of working class mothers on teacher training camps in Chennai decreased when they listened to yoga nidrā. Traumatised military veterans in Washington DC experienced significant reductions in pain from head injuries, and in Petaluma California, thirty elders with sleep disturbances, pain and depression felt their symptoms lift. And these are only seven of the eighty-four studies…

Let us pause to honour this abundance:

49 She who lets elders smile—I honour Her.
50 She who gives sight to the blind—I honour Her.
51 She who gifts hearing to the deaf—I honour Her.
52 She who frees movement and dance in the limbs of the paralysed—I honour Her.
53 She who brings friends to the lonely—I honour Her.
54 She who brings connection to the isolated—I honour Her.
55 She who reclaims breath for the breathless—I honour Her.
56 She who repairs broken limbs—I honour Her.
57 She who soothes broken hearts—I honour Her.
58 She who lets hairs and nails grow—I honour Her.
59 She who cools burns—I honour Her.
60 She who releases the wind from the rectum—I honour Her.

7 Return to resolve, to connect with intuition

And as we circle on in spirals through our pilgrimage in the many realms of Nidrā Shakti, I reaffirm intention here: to join her up, help make her whole. To celebrate her multiples. To sing her pluriverse. To restitute dismemberment and give her this land back. Decolonise, indigenise, and welcome all her kin. Fling wide the doors and let the kith come celebrate our rest. For this is an abundant state to restore our intuition and creativity. As we rest, we become the bed of the ocean of old knowings.

61 She who frees semen to spurt in the dreams of love—I honour Her
62 She who frees menstrual blood to flow from the wombs—
I honour Her.
63 She who holds space for orgasmic ripples of joy—I honour Her.
64 She who lets storms pass—I honour Her.
65 She who gifts fresh perspectives of peaceful revision—
I honour Her.
66 She who gifts sensual dreams of pleasure—I honour Her.
67 She who make enemies friends—I honour Her.
68 She who unifies and levels all inequality—I honour Her.
69 She who must be obeyed—I honour Her.
70 She who makes us stop and lay these bodies down upon the earth—
I honour Her.
71 She who reconnects us to our ancestors through our dreams—
I honour Her
72 She who cannot be resisted—I honour Her.

8 Externalise, contextualise and bring us home again

Please know that every nidrā space is a spacious home for rest. We know this place already, we are resting in her lap. Every night she holds us but we do not honour her. She welcomes us, she lets us enter hypnogogic doors. And every night we rest with her whose name we never knew.

73 She who is ignored at our peril—I honour Her.
74 She who floors the powerful—I honour Her.
75 She who raises up the hearts of the disempowered—I honour Her.
76 She who empowers activists—I honour Her.
77 She who inspires changemakers—I honour Her.
78 She who is the giver of visions—I honour Her.
79 She who brings us home to ourselves—I honour Her.
80 She who opens our hearts—I honour Her.
81 She who lets us snore—I honour Her.
82 She who receives our exhaustion—I honour Her.
83 She who is the bestower of naps—I honour Her.
84 She who signals the start of siesta—I honour Her.

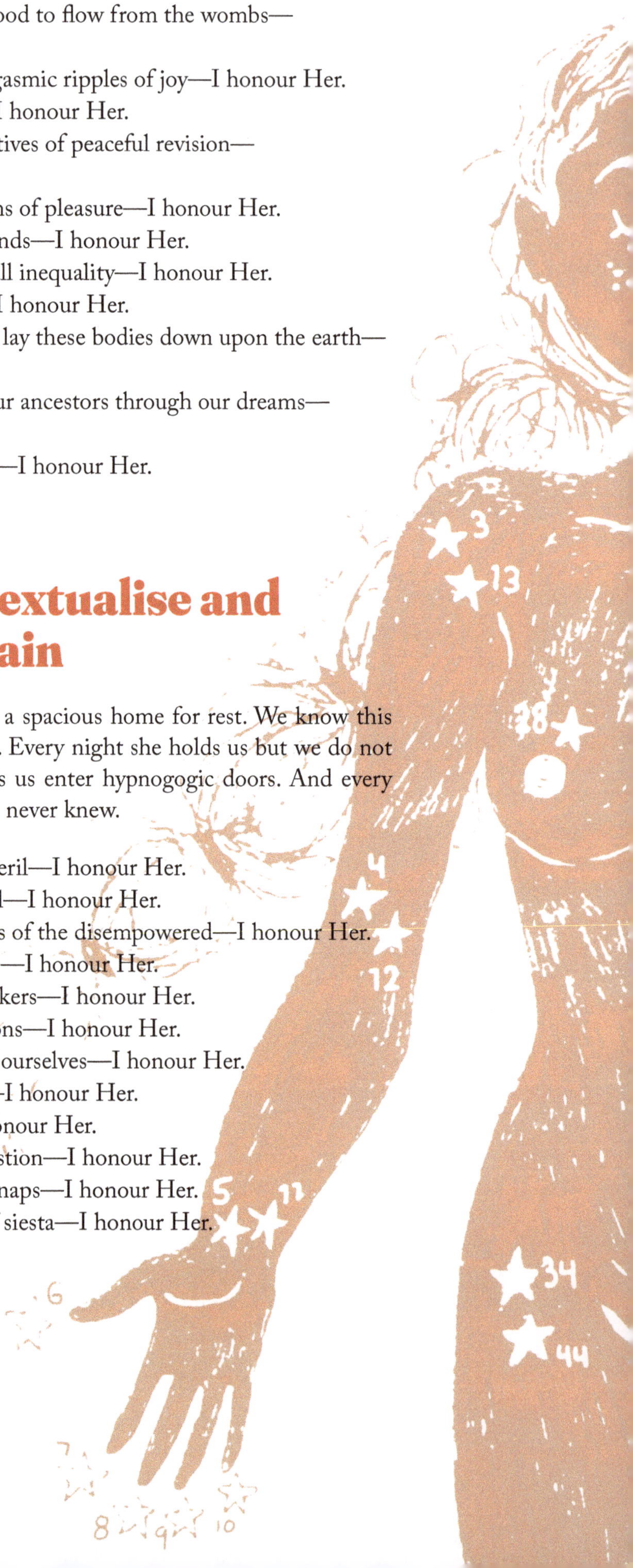

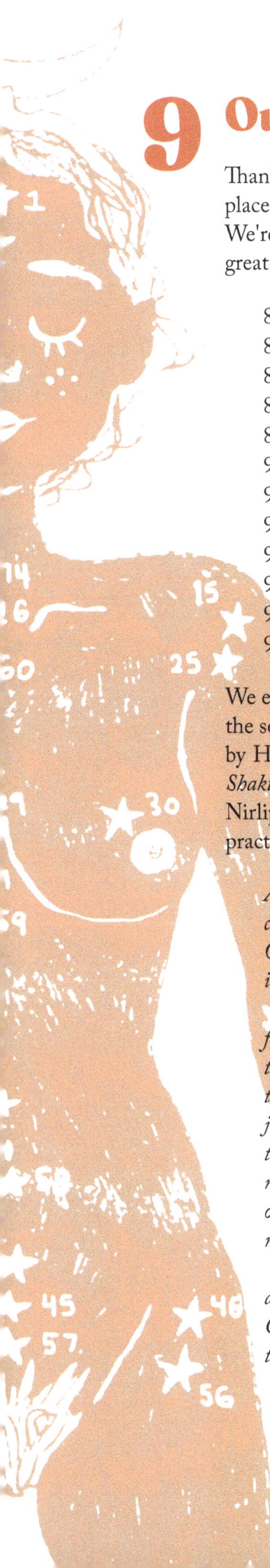

9 Our pilgrimage is made complete

Thank you for accompanying me on this pilgrim trail, for being in this resting place between sleeping and alert. Awaken now, and smell abundance dears! We're rested, here and drenched. We're marinaded, soaked right through. In her great fount our thirst is slaked and word streams overflow.

85 She who quietens even the loudest—I honour Her.
86 She who encourages even the most disheartened—I honour Her.
87 She who is a solace even to the most hurtful abuses—I honour Her.
88 She who gives survivors rest—I honour Her.
89 She who offers respite to carers—I honour Her.
90 She who lets travellers be still—I honour Her.
91 She who offers shelter to refugees—I honour Her.
92 She who dries the tears of the grieving—I honour Her.
93 She who welcomes the excluded—I honour Her.
94 She who embraces the reviled—I honour Her.
95 She who gives the poets words—I honour Her.
96 She who gives the singers songs—I honour Her.

We end with words Nirlipta Tuli spoke about creative flow, how Nidrā Shakti is the source from whence all inspiration flows. Since 1987 he has been nourished by Her and is soaked right to the very bones by that which he calls *the Nidrā Shakti Waterfall: an abundant and endlessly self-renewing fountain of creativity*. Nirlipta is the co-founder of the Yoga Nidrā Network, and from forty years of practice he names from his heart these truths:

> *Abundant creativity is the gift of yoga nidrā… there is so much creativity coming down from Her that if I don't write it down it disappears… but that's OK because there's more—she is abundant. It's like being in a waterfall and it's coming in all directions and very powerfully as well…*
>
> *People talk about a 'stream' or a 'fount' of creativity, and what I have from yoga nidrā is a gushing torrent. If I sit down and write all the creative things that She brings to me, I would not have time to do anything else—and there would be no time to follow through with any of them because there are just so many, and they are so concentrated and potent. There are so many ideas that I have to be ruthless, so that I can just do a few of them well… It took me three weeks to write down over two hundred practices that had arrived on one single outbreath. My main job is trying to get it out of my head and make it understandable to other people.*
>
> *Creativity—this is everyone's birthright. People experience creativity or abundance in different ways—but it is everyone's birthright… Communicating our creativity, the communication doesn't necessarily have to be the language of word. There can be all sorts—music—or cooking or*

gardening, or painting, or whatever—but whatever way we communicate it, we all have it and it is what keeps us human—it's what makes us human.

And we can share our creativity with others without having to do anything—you don't have to go up on the stage and share it. Just being—in your daily activities—just being—*that can communicate this connection to the* waterfall of creativity...

97 She who gives the musicians music—I honour Her.
98 She who strengthens the legs of the runners and the jumpers—I honour Her.
99 She who is an escape for the pursued—I honour Her.
100 She who lets us age with acceptance—I honour Her.
101 She who pauses all wars—I honour Her.
102 She who arrests all conflict—I honour Her.
103 The friend of love—I honour Her.
104 The queen and mother of dream—I honour Her.
105 The sister of rest—I honour Her.
106 The womb of well-being—I honour Her.
107 She who tears apart thought—I honour Her.
108 She who frees us from time—I honour Her.

CODA on Decolonisation and Abundance

This sacred journey has honoured Nidrā Shakti as the abundant and active ingredient of yoga nidrā, a positive force for restoring balance, intuitive interbeing and cyclical rhythmicity. This state we call yoga nidrā nourishes creativity, supports the deepest of healing, and has inspired a bewilderingly astonishing range of remarkable studies, from Wuhan to Los Angeles, and from Edinburgh to Sydney. Our celebratory pilgrimage together has offered glimpses into the marvels of the worlds of yoga nidrā—the yoga of sleep.

Let us speak her name as we complete our pilgrimage around her lands: let us praise Nidrā Shakti and welcome her abundance into our daily lives. In our pilgrimage together here, we have heard her songs... hymns of praise that celebrate our capacity to rest at the edge of surrender into sleep. This is our birthright. Resting as we need is a radical act of reclamation of our capacity to restore and repair ourselves in sleep, to encounter our intuition and creativity, and to be free from the enforced denial of adequate sleep by the inhuman demands of commerce and capital.

I do believe and trust that, in the few remaining places that humans can rest and dream in rhythmic cycles of revival, this power of sleep, Nidrā Shakti, will emerge to heal. In abundant and uncolonised freedom space, at the wild fractal edges of awareness, in the places between sleep and dream, let us remain present enough to hear these songs of freedom calling for repair and restoration.

And how to do that?

Thankfully, it's simple. The best way to encounter Nidrā Shakti is to lay down and listen to Her for yourself, and hear her whisper in your ears, in twenty-three different languages—for indeed her generosity and abundance are legendary. She has a home over here on the Yoga Nidrā Network—*www.yoganidranetwork.org*—look for the free yoga nidrā library—you'll find her there… send her my love as you rest in the abundance of her liminal realm.

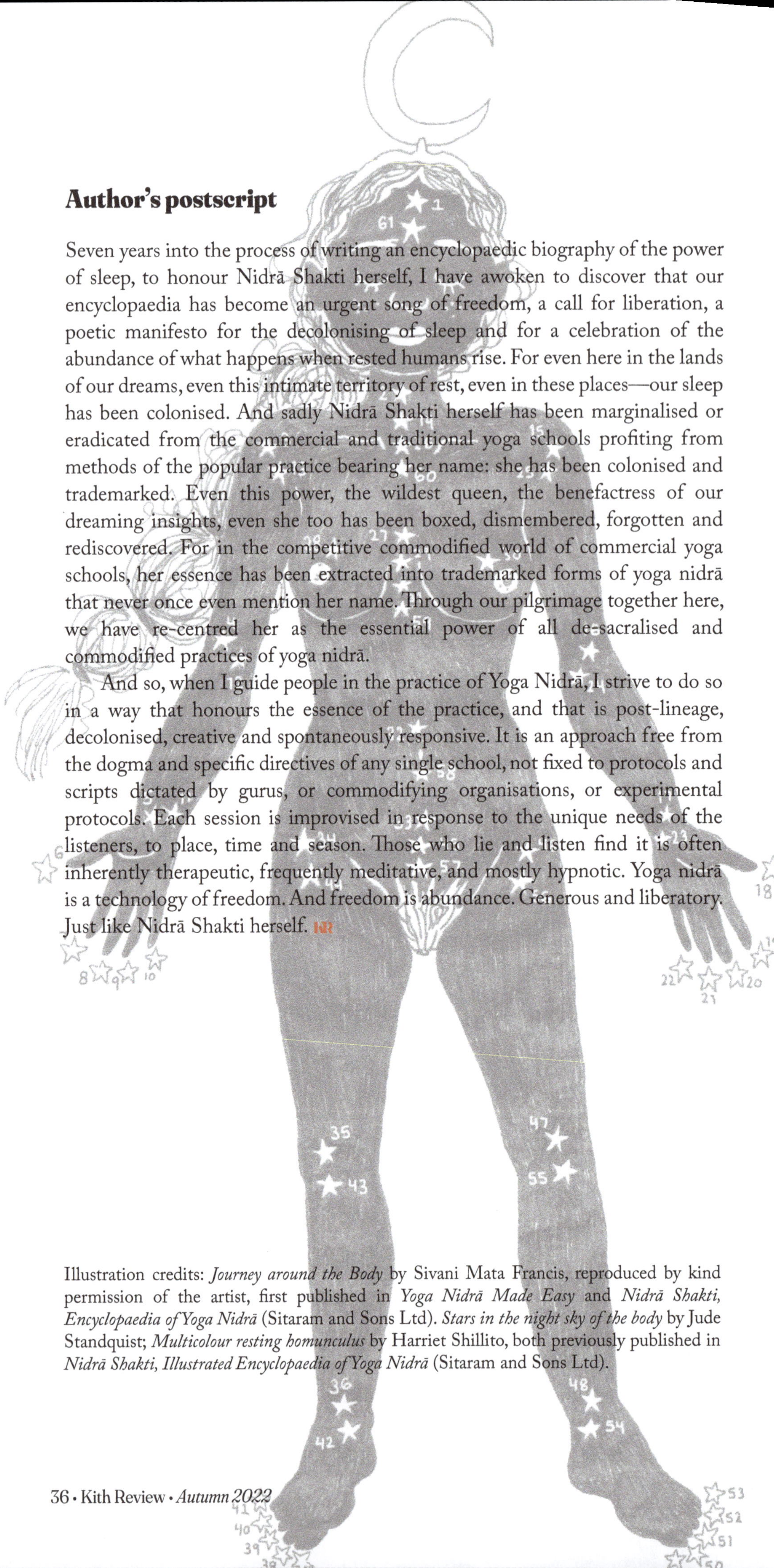

Author's postscript

Seven years into the process of writing an encyclopaedic biography of the power of sleep, to honour Nidrā Shakti herself, I have awoken to discover that our encyclopaedia has become an urgent song of freedom, a call for liberation, a poetic manifesto for the decolonising of sleep and for a celebration of the abundance of what happens when rested humans rise. For even here in the lands of our dreams, even this intimate territory of rest, even in these places—our sleep has been colonised. And sadly Nidrā Shakti herself has been marginalised or eradicated from the commercial and traditional yoga schools profiting from methods of the popular practice bearing her name: she has been colonised and trademarked. Even this power, the wildest queen, the benefactress of our dreaming insights, even she too has been boxed, dismembered, forgotten and rediscovered. For in the competitive commodified world of commercial yoga schools, her essence has been extracted into trademarked forms of yoga nidrā that never once even mention her name. Through our pilgrimage together here, we have re-centred her as the essential power of all de-sacralised and commodified practices of yoga nidrā.

And so, when I guide people in the practice of Yoga Nidrā, I strive to do so in a way that honours the essence of the practice, and that is post-lineage, decolonised, creative and spontaneously responsive. It is an approach free from the dogma and specific directives of any single school, not fixed to protocols and scripts dictated by gurus, or commodifying organisations, or experimental protocols. Each session is improvised in response to the unique needs of the listeners, to place, time and season. Those who lie and listen find it is often inherently therapeutic, frequently meditative, and mostly hypnotic. Yoga nidrā is a technology of freedom. And freedom is abundance. Generous and liberatory. Just like Nidrā Shakti herself. KR

Illustration credits: *Journey around the Body* by Sivani Mata Francis, reproduced by kind permission of the artist, first published in *Yoga Nidrā Made Easy* and *Nidrā Shakti, Encyclopaedia of Yoga Nidrā* (Sitaram and Sons Ltd). *Stars in the night sky of the body* by Jude Standquist; *Multicolour resting homunculus* by Harriet Shillito, both previously published in *Nidrā Shakti, Illustrated Encyclopaedia of Yoga Nidrā* (Sitaram and Sons Ltd).

Marjory Woodfield

Hatshepsut at Deir al-Bahari

On the walls of her mortuary temple
turtles swim in the Red Sea. A heron
catches fish. Domed houses perch on stilts
and date palms line sandy banks.
Men load Hatshepsut's boats

with frankincense, gold, oils, ivory.

They carry myrrh trees up wooden planks,

roots intact. The King of Punt and his wife watch it all.

In Egypt she takes the aromatic bark, incense,
almond oil. White Madonna lilies. Lotus flowers
from her own gardens. Mixes fragrant balms.
She wears the double crown of a unified Egypt.
Regalia and beard of a man. They say her skin
shines like gold. Her face, like stars. KR

Patricia Helen Wooldridge

In the Naming of Things

Warmth, tilting back into summer, mid-July florals
on a quiet Sunday morning—crocosmia splay red,
a blackbird's rest-song, sparrows, chiff-chaff calls.

Winding down, dunnock burst of notes, I had
thought time lurched into autumn, but here's reprieve—
heatful, overgrown, ripe fields, grass-heads

to stroke, ragwort in glory, cinnabar larvae
tiger-striping stems, and in the graveyard, a meadow:
scabious, yellow vetch, purple knapweed to relieve

flutterings of large whites, gatekeepers, and below,
one tattered, marbled white, heyday over from early July—
that windy tidal walk: marsh draining, clouds grown

into ink, stained-glass-wings at my feet, the cry
of kestrel from a hidden nest somewhere in the field-line,
oaks dying into antlers, mud underfoot, mosaic dry,

a yellow-hammer half-song, pineapple weed profusion,
walking over fruited scent beside barley-ripe fur,
ginger on the wind, candy-stripe bindweed to brine

decked with sea-lavender. In a sheltered grove stirs
one dark green fritillary, basking long enough to mind-store
rich flutings, such orange, seeming so much larger

than nearby admirals. Open sea, oystercatcher's en tour
piping. I carry round the names—burweed, dyer's rocket (weld)
thrusting from the banks, viper's bugloss, hedge bedstraw…

To Rain (in June)

Midday in the trickling on/off waves,
blackbird singing in the garden for nearly an hour…

the smell of rain, walking through woods,
leaf mould, stinkhorn, cool air to the river—

hemlock-water-dropwort in overgrown banks,
rain-strings, translucent, soaking into earth,

wide deep puddles on the edge of path
each hollow filling with long absent rain

fennel with its shock of pin-head glass—
I rest and think about water.

This soak, now heavier, moving straight lines, running
into pots, slinking off leaves, the roundness of hazel,

the star-like sycamore, the privet in flower—
detecting scent before seeing… going to school

in a blue check dress, or walking from the station
to work along privet lined path, each a reminder

of others… to here growing wild in the woods,
cool drift in the shadows, and honeysuckle

scrambling over gravel-bed stream—the steady,
run-off, ribbons through the field into

flood-puddle, rush-grass, gathering lake, seeping under
pearl-grey, overhung sky—the blackbird still singing…

Where nothing matters

descending the hill
of Scots pines
into oak woods

the blue stuns…

halting steps while
the wave of scent
sweeps into lungs

how can it be
we didn't know
they were here?

nothing but bluebells KR

Clive Donovan

Birds Sing (in the Woods)

Oh yes, I do remember now, birds sing.
This is what they do. But whose
The unknown hand that squeezes song
And draws the heart from bulbs and sobbing birds and all blithe beasts,
Each contribution flawless as it happens
—Perfect as a picture piece?

Without that nourishment of love and attention
Would they bother to shove into life's
Complexity at all?—the lizards,
The log-munchers and monkey-trick squirrels
And even those casual daffodils over there
Loafing in the breeze…

Whose mind generates the engine of the forest floor?
Whose coaxing eye keeps all the morning moving?
This teeming is sustained in the palm of the one who can hold it,
Even unto these very motes, driven as they are to dance
In shafts of light, defiant of gravity,
Making their homes here as well as us—rightful inhabitants.

But none for too long can endure the pace.
So let us take our turn at ease in the spaces
That we, like sculptors,
Create anew each time we hear
A pureness in the deft note sung,
Notice a leaf ripple in the sun,

This rest we earn after giving so much;
This rest riding on the song of another. KR

unnoticed universes

Photo by Manuel Barroso Parejo on Unsplash

Invisible Abundance

Sarah Watkinson

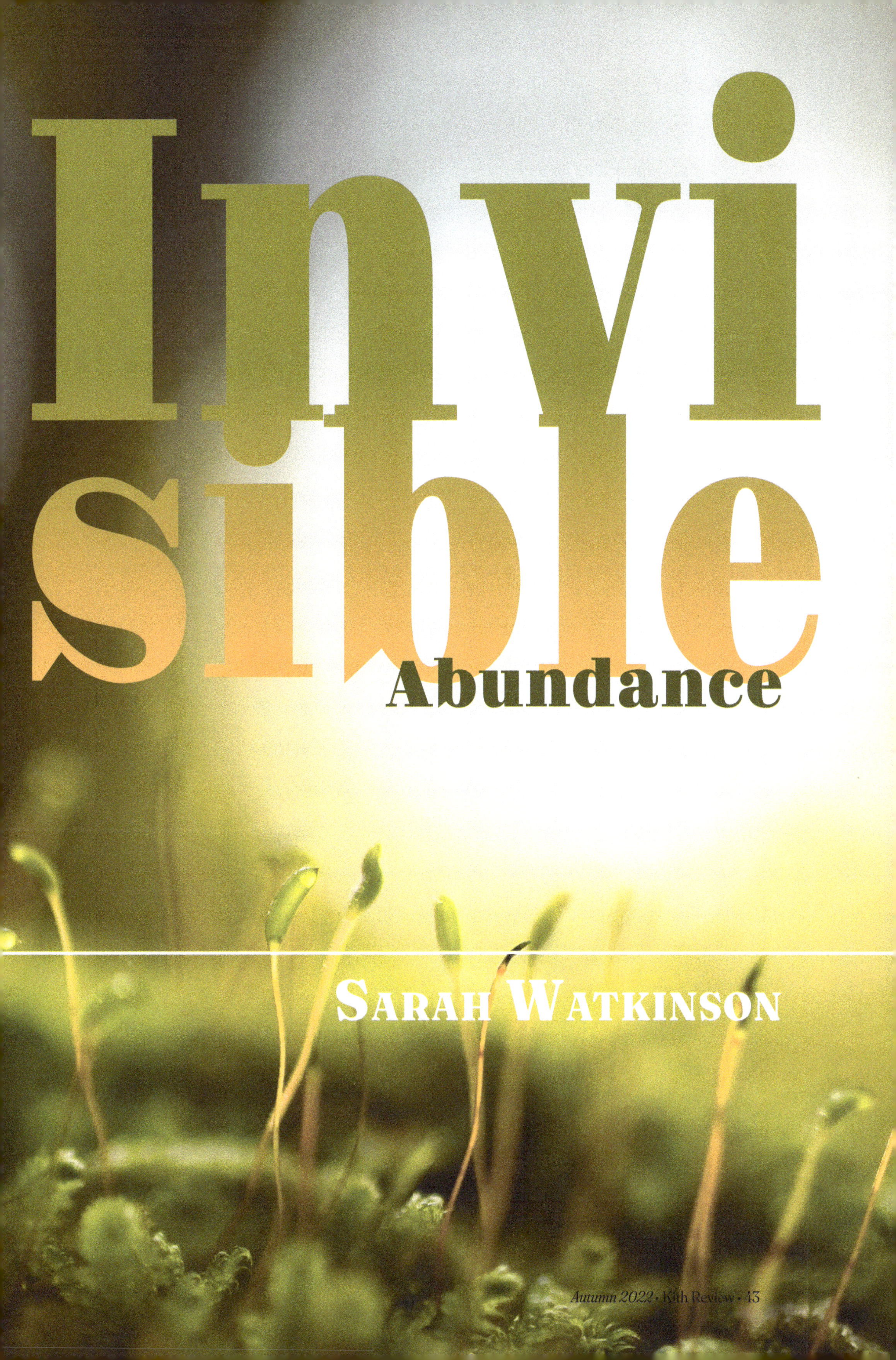

A sense of wonder at the bottomless complexity of our world can suddenly assail you with the force of an epiphany. You might be walking across the city on a November evening and see the lit windows and navy blue sky, the Christmas decorations, cold air, and far off stars, all at once. I love the enigmatic poem by Louis McNeice, 'Snow', for its evocation of this kind of experience. Indoors in a firelit room, it snows outside—and in a strangely euphoric vision you are a speck of conscious life in the vast unknowable universe.

As a young scientist I heard Bob May, as president of the Royal Society of London, deplore the huge budget spent by governments on moonshots when we had hardly begun to catalogue all the species on earth. And how urgent this task was, even back in the nineteen eighties. We were probably losing species that might have been of huge value to us without ever realising their existence. In the days of explorers and *The Jungle Book*, we assumed that nature was inexhaustible. The Genesis version of creation framed nature as a divine gift for humanity to exploit—to have dominion over all other creatures. Only recently have some versions of the Hebrew text translated this as stewardship rather than mastery. The damage has been done, though—complex ecosystems, including the indigenous human inhabitants with the knowledge to curate them, destroyed for intensive monoculture of single species, like oil palm, soya, maize and wheat, traded globally as commodities. Belatedly, we realise we must conserve and restore natural ecosystems for humans to survive on earth; the natural moorlands, mountains, grasslands, forest, peatlands and tundra, oceans and deserts. But we have become fodder for the capitalist Moloch.

Against this apocalyptic background, ecologists realised that there needed to be some objective measure of the amount of wild nature in a landscape, some rule of thumb to triage landscapes for their value in nature conservation. Could we measure biodiversity—the variousness of life in a habitat—without the impossibly laborious task of cataloguing every insect, flower, moss, fungal hypha, bacterium and virus including those not yet discovered?

As readers of Merlin Sheldrake's *Entangled Life* know, fungi underpin all terrestrial life on earth, even though invisible to us for most of the time. They grow within soil or in the bodies of plants or animals, in the form of microscopic hyphae—tip-extending threads. As we walk through a fungus-rich landscape it is only when they emerge for sex that we see enough of them to name, as mushrooms and other recognisable structures. I am a mycologist; fungi are my academic speciality. However, I love natural landscapes and was keen to take part when my university decided that the entire first year of biology students should all be taken into the field to measure biodiversity in nature. We would all go to a field centre in South Wales and we lecturers would demonstrate biodiversity within the students' specialised fields. The great migration would be in the summer term, in late May; not ideal for mushroom hunting, but I was eager not to be left out. In the absence of mushrooms, what could my students measure? There were microscopic moulds, but those, to the uninitiated, mostly look alike and are not very interesting. The one manifestation of fungi in May is in the air, as microscopic spores. With every breath, a person inhales tens to hundreds of fungal spores. They are how moulds spread. In our temperate climate, healthy lungs deal with them; in the allergic or immunosuppressed, and in the tropics, they can cause disease. Technology exists for collecting and identifying them; the Rotorod spore trap is a hand-sized device that whirls sticky arms that spores impact upon, and can then be peeled off and inspected with a microscope. So we had a Rotorod trap made for every student and while others departed for the coast to enumerate guillemots and razor bills, or learned tree-climbing, we investigators of fungal diversity found spores.

What we learned was that even in such small dimensions there was inexhaustible diversity of shapes. Although you couldn't tell their species, you would continue to find occasional new ones for as long as you looked. At first there were new ones in every field of the microscope. If you plot new discoveries against the time spent looking, the curve slopes steeply up as you collect examples of every common type. But the intriguing thing is, that as you persist in the hunt, there are always new shapes among them—scarce rarities continue to accumulate. This is the collector's curve, and it is a rule-of-thumb measure of biodiversity, whatever species you choose to study. For tiny beings, it is valuable, and it proved rather a good way of studying the diversity of fungi in May. You don't need it for large animals. What the collector's curve taught me was that nature is infinitely diverse—as Darwin implied with his phrase, 'endless forms'. The sheer abundance of living forms, specially as you go down into smaller and smaller species, is dazzling. The more you learn, the more interested you become in finding new ones—in rarities. Differences intrigue us. Fishing is addictive, the hunt for rare plants, un-named comets, lost masterworks, gold coins in the earth; the magic of the four-leaved clover and white heather. The search is evidence of the world's complexity—anything could be hidden and might be found. And complexity is the sign of life. Nature, powered by the sun's energy, creates the complexity that is life; a self-perpetuating biosphere of which we are dependent but increasingly destructive members.

> *There is grandeur in this view of life, with its several powers, having been originally breathed into a few forms or into one; and that, whilst this planet has gone cycling on according to the fixed law of gravity, from so simple a beginning endless forms most beautiful and most wonderful have been, and are being, evolved.*
>
> — concluding sentence from *The Origin of Species*, Charles Darwin, 1858

It was Darwin's genius that arrived at the mechanism of natural selection that generates the abundance of forms of life on earth. Janet Browne's 2-volume biography wonderfully describes the background and experiences of this grandson of the Enlightenment that forced him into reluctant and fearful publication of the undeniable truth of evolution by natural selection, and the rejection of the Biblical creation story. I was lucky enough to visit the Galapagos archipelago, and witness the landforms and strange aberrant forms of familiar creatures that live on these geologically new volcanic islands, isolated from each other and from the coast of South America by deep ocean channels.

I pictured the young man, gazing from the deck of *The Beagle*, at what is now Santiago island, and facing a truth which would overturn his own life plan to marry and settle down as rural parson on his return home; and which he knew would destroy the comfortable assumptions of ordinary people. The world was more changeable than they knew— 'crazier and more of it than we think'. I wrote this poem:

Darwin in the Galapagos

Out in the equatorial night,
James Island's long black foreshore is lava—
boiled-over treacle-toffee
just set,
still too new for life.

He sways with the deck's tilt on a Pacific swell.
Alone in the bay
Beagle's riding-light sweeps unknown stars.
Fitzroy has plumbed deep rifts
between the enchanted islands—uncanny,
each the territory of a warped creation.

What immortal hand   Darwin asks,
framed those repellent salt-snot dragons,
neither fish nor lizard
—so strangely un-drownable
and the poor cormorants,
who hold out flightless wings to dry
on baking barrens?

Surviving progeny of long-gone castaways—
or God's a joker.
For proof, he shoots and packs more specimens.
Fitzroy reads the collect of the day.
(*Photovoltaic*, Graft Poetry, 2021)

Richard Dawkins is a masterly exponent of Darwin's thinking, integrating modern understanding of the molecular mechanism of inheritance into Darwin's explanation of the origin of species by natural selection. My favourite of his books is *River out of Eden,* which sees every individual as the inheritor of a unique genome, the assemblage of genes that has come down through their family tree, with all its marriages and new configurations of long-surviving, faithfully replicated but randomly re-assorted genes. The river out of Eden strikes me as a brilliant title that encapsulates our idea of human origins in a rich Edenic landscape, leading to diverging streams of creatures as new geographies shaped endless new forms through time.

Mycologists are very interested in the DNA of the fungi they study, if only because the range of forms is so very limited and yet there is such a huge uncountable number of fungal species in the world. They mostly look alike to us, but have distinct and vital individual roles in ecosystems. They don't photosynthesise, and so, like animals, depend on green plants' ability to capture the sun's energy and steer the captured sunshine into powering the biosphere. Being simple filaments, they feed by growing, and assimilate by dissolving mainly plant material with exuded enzymes. We think of moulds and mushrooms as slow and slimy objects, but at nano-

Photo by Sasha Panarin on Unsplash

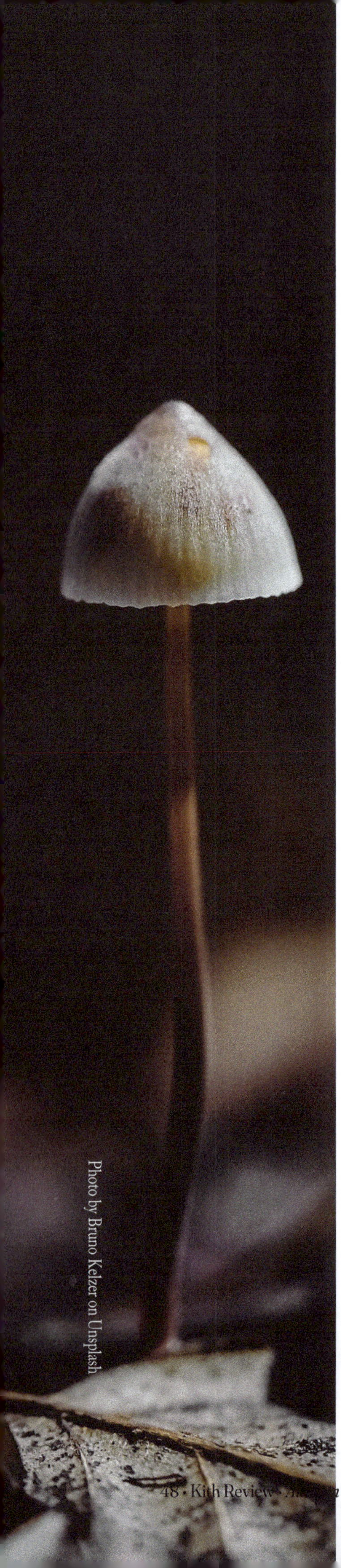
Photo by Bruno Kelzer on Unsplash

scale, like plants, they orchestrate the most violent reactions in biology. They melt wood with a lightning reaction involving free radicals with a nano-second reaction, the most powerful oxidation in a living organism. Fungi are remarkable synthetic chemists, too: thousands of weird organic chemicals are produced, some of which evidently assist the fungus in fighting off competitors for food, or sending signals to coordinate partnerships with other species. Some of these interlock and modify human systems: psilocybin is a promising drug for depression, and statins to control cholesterol, come from moulds in industrial cultures. The repertoire of enzymes to build such exotic substances is inherited and, with modern and fast-developing techniques, mycologists and chemists can find the DNA that codes for the cellular machinery involved.

A fungus with genes that are useful in its habitat is at an advantage, and natural selection will mean that it multiplies, and the advantageous genes will pass into new generations. Where does the dry rot fungus get its remarkable ability from? It's the commonest wood destroying fungus in buildings, but fungi were around long before human buildings. The fungus responsible, Serpula lacrymans, has accompanied my career like a faithful pet. I have attempted to take new directions, but I have always remained interested in this domestic nuisance, and over the years new techniques have emerged to address old problems. Tracing the geographic pattern of its gene evolution, it started as one of many wood rotting fungi in pine woods, growing over the cool damp forest floor from one fallen branch to another. Forming pipes for water and nutrients as it grew over bare soil to meet new wood food bases, it evolved a wood-eating, rapidly spreading way of life. Merchant ships trading between northern European cities and the far east would re-fit and acquire locally sourced masts—pine trees—which would be recycled as domestic building timber in Britain, Japan, or America. These distant origins of dry rot can be worked out from patterns of common genes and human history.

The variousness of fungi underground has long been mysterious, and even more intriguing once we realised that the diversity and productivity of aboveground plants depended on the diversity of mycorrhizal fungi below.

DNA technology was the key that made this complexity accessible and even uncovered the whispered chemical conversations by which fungi and roots forge their mutually advantageous alliances. Nobody has written about this research better than Francis Martin of INRA. *Sous la Forêt* is a wonderful read, as yet untranslated into English, but perfectly possible with my school French; lyrical, deeply informed, cheerfully opinionated, it is the kind of book I would love to read more of: outward-looking, full of delight and wonder and inspired science. Martin's scientific life has been dedicated to the alliances between trees and fungi that sustain forests, their trees, understorey and flowering plants. Fungi tunnel through the soil to feed on sugars from plants, whether releasing them by digesting dead wood or worming their way into the inside of living roots and setting up mutually advantageous exchanges—the plant's sugars made by photosynthesis, exchanged for the fungus's stream of phosphate and potassium plant nutrients. A fungal hypha has multiple capabilities: building a rigid wall behind the thrusting tip, it is like the underground tunnelling machines building the new Crossrail under London; sensing sugar in a root cell, it uses the same biochemistry and the human tongue; forming supply networks of pipes and pumps to scavenge scarce nutrients from the soil, it is a self-organising, resource-responsive network. No wonder a tree 'welcomes' the right hypha into its root tissue, asking for chemical passwords and allowing entrance: then working together, like long-established trading partners, in an exchange of goods that works for both.

Darwin's thinking and observations pre-dated molecular biology and modern chemistry, and the wonder of his great idea is that it works and accommodates our expanding view of smaller and smaller players in the living world: bacteria, protozoa, viruses, even molecules. Ed Yong's book, *I contain multitudes* describes the ecosystem we all carry in our gut, and almost day by day we understand how these bugs can affect not only our digestion but our whole health and even brains. The earth underfoot is full of infinite varieties of molecules—not by accident, but as part of the signals that animals, plants and fungi use. Synthetic chemists learn from and seek out the arcane metabolic pathways coded in microbes, because they can help us. The British Pharmocopeia owes the majority of its pharmacologically active substances to plants and fungi.

Opium, for example, gets picked up by the pleasure-sensing parts of our brain, though it evolved in poppies to deter weevils from feeding on their juice.

Aspirin and Nepenthe

Reward Processing by the Opioid System in the Brain
Le Merrer et al, 2009

Instead of tablets, the nurse gave me a drink
brown and fizzing. The migraine pain stopped.

And more: like a laying on of hands, all was
well
and would be well; I glimpsed a new heaven
and craved a repeat prescription, not for pain
but to escape again, beyond the wall of self.

You tell me opioids aren't simple medicine.
They play on brain rewards, that Nature gave
to make all creatures serve their lines' survival:
deep pleasure, the spring of appetite and
longing.

Morphine's a poppy's weapon against weevils.
I hope, as those bugs taste sour juice, they see
magically, beyond their insecthood,
a wider sky, infinitely good.

Toby Spribille is a mycologist who has used modern analytical techniques to reveal that a beautiful chartreuse-glowing lichen of boreal forest, known in indigenous lore to be effective against wolves raiding the isolated farmhouse, owes its poison to owes its poison to mushroom-related yeast cells that have evolved unrecognised as part of the cooperative microbial assemblage that we cal*l Letharia vulpina*. His paper was published soon after a conversation I had over lunch with the bursar of St Hilda's College, Hikka Helevuo. This prose poem was the result (Litmus, 2021):

The Recipe for Wolfbane

For Hilkka Helevuo

You told me about your winter journey; how, after long hours on the main road from Helsinki, you would turn the car on to a single track through forest, down to your ancestral place, two miles along the lake shore at the peninsula's end. How the headlights' bright tunnel through the dark was walled around with curtains of lichen glowing green and white on the old spruce trees. How this was always a home-coming, to the *mökki* you named *Tyttola*—the daughters' house. I imagine the stars, and the cold, and the resined air sifting through the draped branches. The cabin is icy, quiet, woody; you light a fire, eat and drink. You are all there for Christmas, alone and happy in the clean air.

Photo by Jaap Straydog on Unsplash

I am wondering if that green glow that spoke to you of home was the chartreuse shine of wolf-bane, *Letharia vulpin*a, the reindeer lichen's toxic gold-green twin, the pair so alike in all but colour that no-one could discover what held code for that gold poison, sovereign against the predator slinking into the yard, until Spribille unspooled the spell. With new primers written in old mushroom tongues, he found the wolf-lethal cells of a primeval yeast, shielded from diagnostic beams by the slimy core, transcribing their old vulpinic acid recipe from sequences invisible to conventional taxonomy.

Darwin's 'great idea'—natural selection as the machinery of life's complexity-generating machine—pre-dated molecular biology. It is a witness to Darwin's genius that it works at the invisible level of chemistry, unthought of in his day. DNA technology and analytical chemistry reveal wonders of cooperation and interaction among the five kingdoms of life on Earth. Over aeons, the collaborations that grow from chemical conversations produce new lives and new identities. Lichens arose when soil fungi recruited photosynthetic algae (cells such as those that make that green slime on wet tree trunks and shady rocks) into their tissue, so they could emerge from the dark underground and feed themselves on sunlight. Lichens turn out to be far more that dual partnerships; they are communities of tiny organisms, each of which may bring a unique attribute to the whole.

Humans are intensely dependent, but we fool ourselves that we can go it alone. This great delusion is fostered by our alienating Anthropocene environment. We have grandiose and over-reaching expectations of technology, dazzled by the digital world. Our 'photovoltaic arrays' are childish meccano, no substitute for the sophisticated miniaturisation of a leaf, inside which a tiny, violent photovoltaic reaction converts air, water and sunlight into a beautiful edible object—the shortest food supply chain ever. We need to tell our children an updated creation story, one that learns appropriate awe at the extraordinary and hardly-understood miracle of life; a sunlight-driven, complexity-generating system unique in the universe as far as we know.

The Wood-Wide Web

Antiphon to 'Mould Music', Philip Gross

Underfoot, sharers
in the earth,
with one tree
or another,

they grow nets
to catch salvage:

scatterings of wood,
washings of foliage...

store and return salts, for a fee
paid in summer sap.

They whisper their way
into roots, and become

chimaera: *Mycorrhiza*,
rufous, violaceous, melanised,
down in the dark.

Stinkhorns, earthstars,
deceivers, chanterelles—

their spore-launchers—come up
in their own time, in warm damp.

They deal us whatever helps them:
disgust, death, delicatessen, musk. KR

Denise Steele

Coulter's Wood

Lonely for friends, I walk at dusk
where cows come down to water.
Last night I watched them gulp and drip,
wrap and pull great rasps of grass,
finick willowherb over the fence.

Tonight just a distant bellow or two,
an antiphon of fretting sheep,
a rabbit's softness lolloping past,
fur silver in a mist of rain—
the scent of wet to dampen thirst.

Then on the home path suddenly
            —you—
three light bounds to pause, head-turn.
Sizing me up you ask my view,
calmly finish a trailing mouthful.
Eye to eye I drink us in. KR

Sr Sally Witt

A Nation Needing Silence

This morning
the cardinal
perched on a branch in our alley
did not sing.

I've heard his varied calls before.
This morning
did he know
we are a nation needing silence,

maybe even his?

Wings of Stillness

for the Sisters of St. Joseph of Watertown, New York

Your days combine great works with simple acts
of worship, welcoming the stranger, washing dishes.
Fashioning the earth in needle points of colour,
you are faithful to a deep, rushing prayer.

So, at the time of day
when the sun turns into liquid brilliance
and drips behind the mountaintops,

when clouds fall into pink and purple layers,
forming beauty after beauty in the changing light,
set aside the book of prayers, the dishpan.
Come to watch magnificence of evening.

This is your prayer translated into colour,
your faithful, daily prayer
that runs to God on wings of stillness.

The book and dishpan will return,
but for these sunset minutes
see the longing of your soul
embraced by God.

Making a Life

Andrea Turner

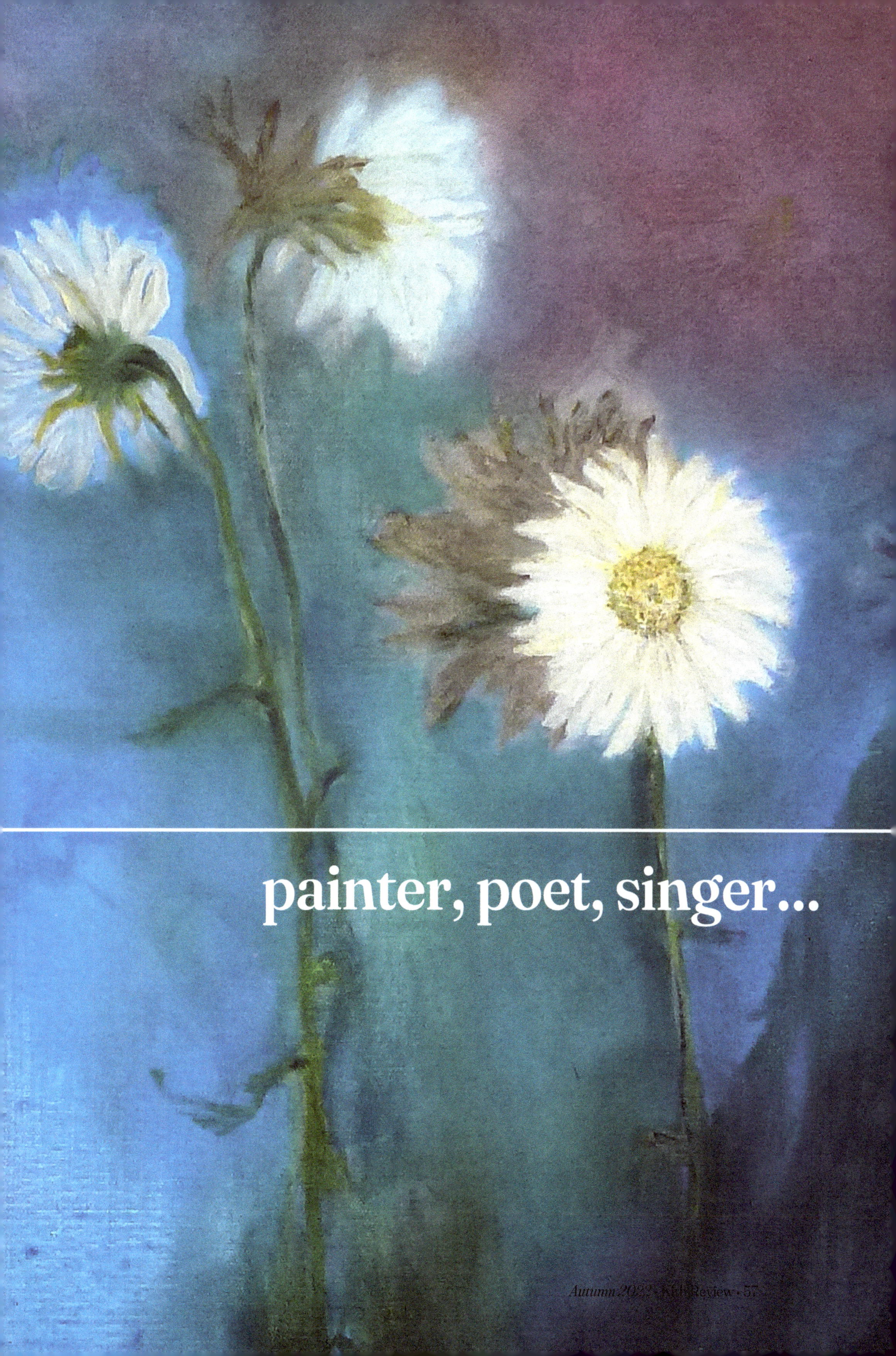

painter, poet, singer...

The Music of Painting

Find a photograph of seven darting fish,
cut out their bodies, transfer them to a screen.
Push the squeegee pull paint through the stencil,
colour blends, each layer pristine.

A fiddler says *the process is like music*
I'll transpose colours, draw them on a stave,
harmonies in thirds and fifths and sevenths,
choirs will sing the melodies I engrave.

In the descant I see a painting,
stretch a rigid frame with drum-tight cloth,
prime the ground with glue composed of rabbit skin,
then a wash of oils, hand fast and loose and rough.

Something swims within that first blotched coating,
I catch, lose, reel it in again.
Ask question after question of the canvas,
answers are unveiled with brush and pen.

Dipping in a Scarlet Lake of pigment
I pick out details, add glazes, texture, stains.
Colours sing in concert and discordance,
some breach, bleed beyond their frames.

The painting tells a story of its making.
If you want images here's osprey, poppy, birch.
A river flowing full across the centre.
Some marks that can't be read, they might be words.

Someone once asked me what I do and I told them I paint, sing, write poetry. I said I make only half a living and she replied, 'but I think you make a life.' This wisdom from a stranger landed deep within me and has become a touchstone when things are materially tough, which is pretty much always. I know I'm making my life.

Making art is hard, it's frequently unpaid. For every success story ringing from the tannoy of social media there are literally hundreds of creative people quietly getting on with their work, scraping by, reliant on teaching, part time jobs, their partners wages, parental handouts, silver spoons or benefits. It is the gifted/lucky/driven few who find themselves able to spend their lives making art and nothing else.

And yet, I'm aware there are other choices. When I left school, although I was being encouraged to apply for art college by my teachers, I chose nursing, one of 3 options apparently open to me as a young woman living in a small village near Glasgow in the late 1970s: 1: Get married—almost but not quite, 2: move away—eventually! 3: go into nursing—tick.

I spent 16 years working on acute medical wards and acute psychiatric wards. For 12 of those years I worked nights part time while studying for a BA (Fine Art) at Goldsmiths College in London and spent my days making art. I lived in a housing association flat for NHS workers in Camberwell with 3 other women, my rent was £7 a week. I moved to a squatted 'hard to let' council flat when they became separatist feminists and it became challenging for me to have my boyfriend over. We stayed friends but it was time to move on.

As a group of artists and musicians we took over a derelict shop on the Old Kent Road and turned it into studio space. The 1980s were a time when it was possible, in England at least, to find living and working space for free. We did places up, paid for utilities. My greatest luxury then and now was time to explore my thoughts and ideas, time to make creative work, to feel a sense of freedom and possibility in my life.

In 1988, with London growing weary of me, I packed my belongings and my art materials and got on a train to Inverness. I landed in a friend's cottage, a sublet while she moved to the world famous eco village of the Findhorn Foundation. It was December 15th, there was one coal fire for heating and a broken window that allowed the warm smoky air to escape and replaced it with air as cold as stars. The cottage was in a field on the edge of the ancient Darnaway Forest. My neighbours lay on the grass sweating and snoring, great clouds of steam rising from their flanks. In the morning a vast bull threw his bulk over an indifferent cow and impregnated her inches from my bedroom window.

Change Tempo

Andante

I cross the minor road with an easy stride,
one bridge to another, linger on verges

wild with poppies, cowslip, broom.
A palette of sky blue, scarlet, yellow

paints a recollection of childhood,
of frogs and caterpillars, wasps and bees.

Rubato

Let's steal away
from the metronome
enter time's funhouse
twist and swell
in ill-tempered mirrors
pitch and reel on the cakewalk
scatter like pearls
through the barrel of love

Adagio

Ballad of a song thrush at the rowan's crown.
Duet of osprey on spiralling air.

Black the night-wide river.
Gold the moon-mirrored cloud.

Rain splashes toothed leaves of a horse chestnut.
Conkers unlash their burnished eyes.

Vivace

A pearl quivers, sprouts wings, claws, beak,
hatches a kingfisher—dart in the seam.

Sparrows nest in the gutters above my window,
flit from sill to fence, sing.

Starlings swoop through the yard
where a sycamore once greened out the horizon.

Footfall • watercolour by Andrea Turner

Identification of myself as Artist, the full embodiment of that archetype, has taken me many years and involved diversification of my original practice as a painter, firstly into music and more recently into writing poetry. Over time these aspects of my creative work have become aligned so that they now feel parts of the whole; facets of one creative expression which can work as individual disciplines but are increasingly working together.

Music has been a central part of my life from a very young age. But by studying music in my late 30s, learning the language and the repertoire, learning how to play my chosen instrument—the voice, I gained another form of expression and felt a great balance between the solitary life of a painter and the communal life of a collaborating musician; able to move between silence and sound, solitude and community in my work.

More recently I have started writing poetry. Writing has been part of my artistic practice for a long time and I have often preferred to describe the world in words rather than in sketch form. Again, for me, it has been the focused study and practice of writing that has brought poetry into the core of my creative practice.

For me abundance is the fulfilment of a creative impulse, the feeling I get when fully engaged in my creative work, when my thoughts are focused on colour, mark, music, words and I am placed at the centre of this maelstrom as choices kaleidoscope around me.

Frame

My fingertips graze across remnants
of scallop, leaf, tendril, flower,

probe facets, discs and joints,
as if sculpting the vertebrae of my unborn's spine.

I can't say how many hours pass,
only that the light from my lamp is constant

and, in glancing up at the window,
the light is always changed.

Wolf moon rises, frost scalds the fields,
under the anglepoise plaster dust glimmers.

In this starred and owled night
I close my eyes to read more deeply.

A hand slips around mine.
Three hundred years between us, still he finds me;

the maker of this frame, called through centuries
by my scratching at the door of inspiration.

The pattern reaches into our hands
Flowers bud, tendrils unravel, scallops fan open

as if the heartwood remembers its form
has been longing for a greening touch.

In the final act I lay goldleaf over our restoration
and he flits like a dragonfly on the tides of my breath.

River Sun • watercolour by Andrea Turner

I still live in North East Scotland, although I took a diversion and moved to Edinburgh for 10 years when my children were small. Essentially I feel that I live in both places: my physical home is Forres, my cultural home is Edinburgh. It was in Edinburgh that I stepped into the world of singing and performance, immersed myself in Edinburgh's rich jazz scene and put on shows at the Edinburgh Festival Fringe. I also maintained an art studio in a wonderfully focused and enlivening studio block housing about 40 artists of varying disciplines. We were all involved in making art, our passions in the details of layering paint or creating form. There was always someone to chat with at the communal sink, someone to ask for feedback from if I had been working so long on a painting I could no longer see it clearly. Always a cup of coffee at the end of the road or a trawl round the second-hand shops when I needed a break.

When I moved back to Forres in 2008, arriving in yet another cold, damp cottage, I returned to the studio I had left years earlier. Instead of cafés there are trees, in place of second-hand shops—tractors and cows. These situational changes have had a profound effect on my work. Being surrounded by such voluptuous natural beauty was initially challenging. I wondered what I had to add to the great art that nature provided. What I could say that wasn't already being said more completely by the trees, rivers and beaches. I thought about the visceral relationship of the farmers to this land. Questioned the authenticity of my own incomer's voice.

Clarity has come through writing. Writing allows me to explore my relationship to the landscape and, through minute observation and documentation, come to know it. Not only as a place of vast beauty following its own cycles of life and death, but also as a place of subtle shifts and interior spaces. This detailed enquiry also allows me to come closer to myself, to understand and know the subtle parts of my own being.

The following 2 pieces of writing are taken from my newest project—Small Wood—a series of monthly Haibun written throughout 2021.

February

Quartz and Opal

I tread the chiselled, marble land. Every twig a fork of snow, every leaf a spoon of light. The air smells of mountains. At the burn, gallop of whisky-amber water falters on a spangled bank. I dip away. There is no singing. A sudden squall and high above, pine-masts creak, flex like wheat. Roots hold firm, wind barred by every strut and keel of branch and trunk. I would crawl inside a hollow stump shawled in cobwebs and Lichen until the thaw. My bones are sleet.

Each Swan-white crystal;
plume of tufted cloud. Snowfall's
quiet weight of grace.

June

Tipping Point

Leave me be. I'm grounded here. Eyes alert. Ears fine-tuned; thrilled by trills. I dance between earth-ravelled trees. Swallow windblown seeds. Let wood-scribes write within me. I'm seeking conversation, not monologues or contemplation. Redwood, were you consulted on your rootless relocation? My feet swerve foxglove, harebell, grass as I leave the scuffed, unseeded path. I shed desire like pollen, undress all expectation. How long before the fall occurs? Water alone laps silt from bedrock. Only stone clocks shave dust from time.

To hear: *first listen*
To speak: *silence sifts your tongue*
To See: *stun your eyes*

As my observations of and interactions with the natural world have become increasingly sensitive, questions about my fitness to comment have receded. Much is made of our belonging in a place. Worlds are dis-ordered around how we sound, how we look, but there are places beyond this, in our deep relationship with nature which, to me, feel more real, more authentic and more alive. It is these places I am trying to reach through my work. KR

Links:
soundcloud.com/andreaturner/you-brought-the-mountains-to-me
soundcloud.com/andreaturner/my-love-is-like-a-red-red-rose-by-robert-burns

Imblued • oil on canvas by Andrea Turner

Marc Harshman

Ruach

The wind high up on a leafless day in early spring
        is carrying all the air I could ever need.
A few small clouds of sheep follow unaware of my need.
A whistle echoes uniformly three times
        throughout the hour within the blackberry patch.
        Whose? How? Why?
        Towhee, oriole, grosbeak?
I cannot answer, though this, here, perhaps an attempt?
The shape of the continent slowly draws its shadow
        down the rump of my virgin lawn.
Its map is speckled with new cities as yet unknown, unnamed, unvisited
        except by the last, heroic bees who name them, as I do, white violets.
I go on, then, believing that what I have in common with the world matters
        and this breath, at least, was, and will go on being
        worth the bother of all approaching storms.

Note: 'Ruach' has various spellings but as the Hebrew noun *ruach* it can refer not only to the Holy Spirit but also to breath or wind.

The Old River Still New

Isaiah 43: 18-19

The brown river, heavy with the weight of recent flood,
drags its way through these ancient hills.
A mist-smudged mini-rainbow wavers blue and pink
above the waters' slow passage south.
I'd like to imagine that it is in a moment like this,
in a light made perfect by May's endless rehearsals
that Christ would wend his way back to us,
not with the unasked foolish and false prophets,
their swords and hate, but with his simpler testimonies,
the storytelling, the finger in the sand, the water
become wine, a wand of blossoms
and words sweet as the honeysuckle now
wreathing the far bank of this living river.

Almost a Translation

In Memoriam: Ruth Calway

It's a short, warbling burst of only seconds but still I look
    and on the electric line against a slate sky is a small,
    chalk-blue bird, chest smudged a rusty-peach,
    who's called to me and then,
    out of the corner of my eye,
    another swings invisibly into view.
It's enough to make me think there's always more
    than the day's troubles, enough to make me breathe
    and look about me, sift through the green
    of the hillside, imagine the trembling whispers
    of the leaves as the wind lifts, and begin to believe
    if I sit here long enough I might
    even translate that whispering, learn
    exactly what that one bluebird
    was saying to the other.

Suzanna Fitzpatrick

The Correct Way to Greet a Tiny Thing

a pyralid moth, say
or the goldcrest, Europe's smallest bird
or anything velvet with feathers

is to raise a forefinger slowly and gently

perhaps a harvest mouse, its long pink toes
tipped with claws the thickness of one of your hairs

in which case whisper, minimising vibrations

or maybe the common pipistrelle
its heartrate rapid as static

then dim all lights, shutter your eyes' shine

and remember everything eats the minnow
so cause no ripple, even with your breath

but simply nod. Acknowledge. That is best. KR

J V Birch

The tap

is one of those push down ones but it's broken
because someone's twisted
the top off so there's nothing to push down
and as the water's gushing
out into the cracked enamel sink and I'm thinking
what a waste this is a whale
plops out and starts singing followed by some fish
and a turtle who tells me
about the creatures we'll meet when everything's
flowed over and as I watch
them swimming and spinning I turn the tap off
at the mains because
we're not quite
ready yet. KR

Mick Evans

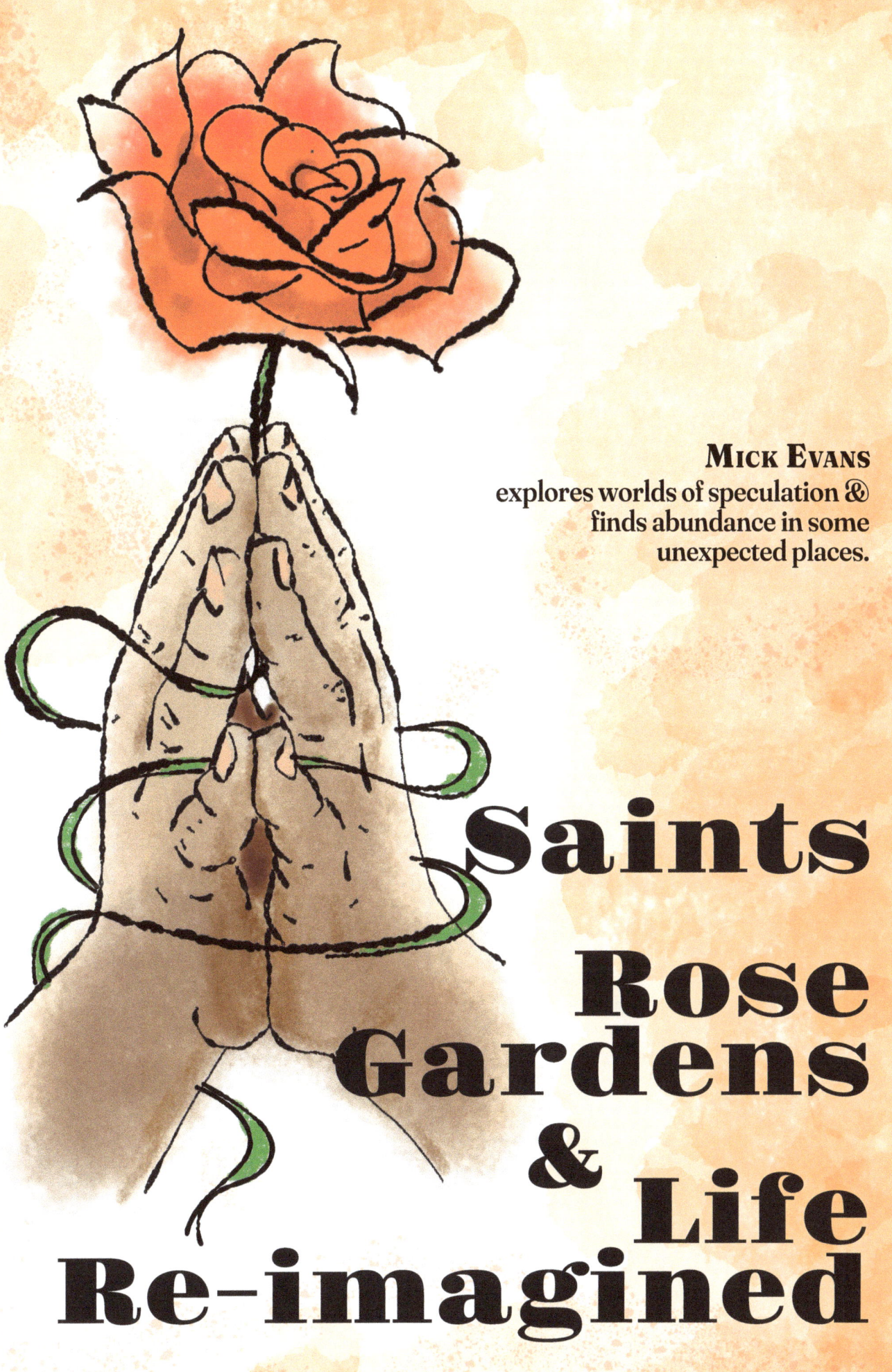

explores worlds of speculation & finds abundance in some unexpected places.

Saints Rose Gardens & Life Re-imagined

I once unwittingly revealed my ignorance to a friend, a devout orthodox Catholic, when I said St George was not a real person. He put me straight. More importantly, he asked a significant question: 'Why should a saint need to be a real person?'

I had no answer, but those who study myth will have. One point about abundance is that artists and narrative makers bring an entirely valid existence to the imagined. It is the privilege and great opportunity of artists to pursue unlived lives, and give them a truth, 'a local habitation and a name'. In that respect, the artist's subject matter is infinite, and infinity.

Eliot's *Four Quartets* begin, in Burnt Norton, with a positing of this: because all time is unredeemable, and other possible existences contained within it, imagining becomes a moral and humanitarian act 'only in a world of speculation'. They are a 'perpetual possibility' only in that domain. 'What might have been and what has been' form an infinite and eternal dimension of existence: our greatest abundance. Our lost ones exert their desire and need for existence not only in memory, but through the imagination. Biographers may tell us a great deal about that relationship. The ancestors conduct their constant conversation with us: they are so much ourselves, it is often impossible to distinguish them within our individuality.

A critic once spoke of 'the infinite destinations of the soul' in Samuel Beckett's short poem 'Saint-Lô'. Beckett describes a town destroyed by bombardment after D-Day as the 'capital of the ruins'. It suffered such extensive damage that the river Vire running through it changed its course. That new direction and the ruined town become a potent metaphor for the unborn and yet redeemed. Their tenuous link to our world of experience is captured brilliantly in his use of the word 'tremble': a state frail yet awe inspiring, alive, dynamic, and independent, within the world of possibility. I quote his quatrain in full:

Vire will wind in other shadows
unborn through the bright ways tremble
and the old mind ghost-forsaken
sink into its havoc

Our paths not taken are into the lives not lived that 'through the bright ways tremble'. The writer's quest leads into this otherness.

In 'Burnt Norton Eliot' takes the imagery of the rose garden from Kipling's story, *They*. The narrator finds himself in the beautiful garden of a blind woman. He is haunted by the sound of running feet and children hiding in the bushes. He comes to realise these are the ghosts of children drawn to the woman who is unable to bear children herself, but loves them deeply. The narrator has lost a child , and discovers she is among them, through a poignant secret signal. It seems almost superfluous to add that Kipling was working out a personal grief. Though the story is one of deep sadness, there is an abundance of joy in the woman's love that draws the children to her, her 'eternal possibilities', and a moment of redemption for the stricken narrator.

AE Coppard's story, 'Adam and Eve and Pinch Me' tells of a husband who falls into a parallel existence where he becomes invisible and unable to communicate with his family. During a troubled afternoon, he encounters the future in the angelic form of his unborn son.

Both these stories deal in different ways with lives unlived, but held eternally as possibilities within the world of human experience. I return to my friend's unsettling question: Why should a saint need to be a real person? Is our immediate reality the only valid one? The sheer abundance of possibility that opens in that view is breathtaking.

The invention and interpretation of the otherness of experience is the matter and business of poetry: tentatively but full of hope, we enter the realms of wonder. If we are fortunate, we may share the overwhelming sense of sheer abundance of possibility that literature offers, in the 'wild surmise' of Keats' 'On first looking into Chapman's Homer'. We may never know the physical reality of the imagined lives of those who inhabit the rose garden, but we may stir the leaves and hear them rustle. KR

Adam Craig

The Summer house

every season can feel like winter

Karl glanced up at the summerhouse and caught a glimpse of something lingering in its warped timbers and shedding roof. The autumn afternoon was turning cold, its grey hands hiding the sun to cast a foreshadow of approaching winter. The days were fast shrinking, another year slipping by. Vaguely disturbed by the thought, Karl shrugged more deeply into his jacket. Taking a firmer grip on the rake, as if trying to anchor himself in the present, he went back to work only to look up again after a few minutes.

The summerhouse stood, half-hidden behind a screen of bushes in the far corner of the garden. The cold lessened at the sight of the building, replaced by a whispering of green leaves and an impression of dappled sunlight falling across his face. Rather than approaching dusk, each breath was suddenly filled with the mingled scents of peony and honeysuckle.

Karl shook his head: *It's just an abandoned hut*. No matter how often he thought that, he could not quite convince himself it was true. There was something about the summerhouse, something that managed to conjure up an aftertaste of summers gone.

Diligent and steady, he let the rake slip out through his hands to gather a fresh pile of leaves. Only a few stragglers remained to be collected and he would be done. Instead, Karl found himself pausing again. Gazing up the garden to the large, copper-roofed house. A pair of French windows stared back emptily.

No sign of Miss Clara today.

Sometimes, she stood in her grandfather's study, looking out of the windows down the length of the garden. Clara said little, her reserve as deep as Karl's. Still, he could not help noticing how she often stared towards the summerhouse as it peeked over the screen of trees. Nor could he help wondering if she was searching for the same thing he saw in the little building.

Decisively, he pushed the thought away. The shadows pooling around the trees standing along the edges of the garden were growing ever deeper. It was time he returned to work. With simple economy, he drew the last catch of leaves towards his feet. Like a fisherman casting his net. At least, that was how he thought of it. Karl had never seen the sea, except in the cinema, although he imagined the copper roof of the main house might be the colour of the ocean.

The sun, chin almost on the horizon, peered curiously from a gap in the clouds, ruddy face visible between the trees as Karl filled the wheelbarrow. He trundled back and forth until the pile of ash beyond the summerhouse was once again hidden under fallen leaves. Standing back, he wetted a finger to confirm the gentle breeze would carry stray sparks away from the frail hut. Satisfied, Karl dug his father's old lighter from a pocket.

Fire leapt from leaf to leaf, detouring around those too damp to catch, only to come back and embrace those, too. Musky smoke coiled through the damp air. Night drew closer, the sun slipping under the horizon to leave the bonfire to burn alone. Finding its voice, the fire spoke to the darkened garden. Dry whispers of long, warm days and a golden season already beginning to seem a distant memory as autumn dressed everything in russet and auburn.

Karl looked back towards the summerhouse. Fire-glow touched its walls, bringing temporary life to the weathered boards and missing shingles. Like this, it was easy to see it as it had been, when his father had been gardener here and Clara had been—what? Younger, anyway. Miss Clara surely must only be a few years older than Karl.

Soon, the bonfire dwindled until only a few embers remained, glowing faintly like the stars overhead.

Buttoning his jacket against the cold, Karl walked up the garden. Thoughts ran ahead to bring images of dinner and an evening silent but for the ticking of the clock and the crack of wood smouldering in the grate.

At the corner of the house, he paused to examine its dim face. There was no sign of Clara.

Winter came to press its face at every window in the house.

Clara paused at the bottom of the broad staircase. A wind toyed with the great copper tiles on the roof, then scurried away. The old house, used to such things, groaned mildly and resettled itself. Clara turned. Doors, mostly half-open, led off the hallway. A shaft of reticent light paused in each one, grey fingers lying across their lips, requiring silence.

Silence filled the house, deepening as the season deepened. Clara moved with care. Pale hand against a brass doorknob made smooth by the caress of other hands long gone, she pushed open the door to her grandfather's study. The hinges turned noiselessly.

Most sounds felt like intruders into the stillness of the house. Certainly any reminder of the world outside—whether the gentle soughing of the wind or the clatter of hail against the glass—struck Clara as being unwelcome. She often found herself straining to ignore their distraction. Instead, she listened beyond these interruptions for something hidden in the building's natural silence. Sometimes, Clara was positive she caught a snatch of muted conversation coming from beyond a half-closed door, or soft footfalls other than her own.

Yet, she was alone in the house. Her only company was the emptiness that lingers when someone steps from a room and if she heard anything at all, it could only be a memory of something long gone.

She crossed the room to sit at the desk used by her father and grandfather. Selecting a sheet of writing-paper, Clara uncapped her fountain pen and let the nib hover. Winter was a time for memories, the time when she wrote to those few school friends who still kept in touch. Slowly, conscious of the gentle scratch of nib on paper, she began to write. A single letter to each, filled exclusively with remembrances: do you remember when? who was it who? On the subject of the present, she was always vague. The present was something she could barely grasp, let alone discuss.

Clara gazed at the unfinished sentence and realised that, today, even the act of repeating the past was too difficult.

Restless, she moved from room to room, each voiceless, their eyes closed as the softly creaking floorboards inevitably led her back to the study. Letters abandoned, she took up her knitting. Scarves for the children in the infant's school, just as her mother had done, her grandmother also. Clara had no talent for knitting. Some winters, she finished only one scarf before Christmas, her labours wrapped in paper and ribbon and passed to Karl for delivery.

Still she knitted. Eyebrows drawn together, a frown of concentration collecting shadows, Clara worked laboriously. The *tick* of needle on needle felt oddly permissible, not really an intrusion into the house at all. Her mind drifted back, searching out those times when the broad staircase had known the tread of more than just one woman, and the high-ceilinged rooms had resounded to near-constant use.

In amongst those memories, she turned over images of summer days. Sunlight pooling on the outstretched leaves of the horse-chestnut, spilling between its jade fingers to sparkle in the shade under swaying branches. A butterfly flexing its wings, holding them wide to reveal sapphire eyes that gazed up at an unbroken blue sky. The old lawnmower gently whirring as Karl's father wrote another stripe down the narrow lawns between brimming flowerbeds. A bee dipping into magenta and lilac asters. Karl himself, younger than she, peering around the open doorway into the summerhouse. Reading, playing, talking away the hours. In the summerhouse…

Hands fumbling, a stitch dropped free. Clara paused. Silence stood beside her. Each memory of summer was fading into the quiet, colours tending towards sepia. And, as the memories dimmed, so all sense of this house being her home slipped away.

Now it's a prison. The thought made her sag.

Silence rested a hand on her shoulder, the house pressing closer. She felt powerless to leave. Even stepping between the French windows into the garden was difficult. Walking down hill to the centre of the town seemed impossible. No, it was impossible and had been ever since the house began echoing to sounds and events long past.

Clara put aside her knitting and pulled the tottering card-table closer. A sheaf of astrological tables and charts, corners curling over, lay heaped in one corner, an unfinished spread of Tarot cards taking up the rest of the shabby baize.

Hands shaking with need, she turned on the record player. The hesitant opening of the Goldberg Variations gently pushed back the silence. Bach filled the room and, if only until the record finished, she could believe there was something other than ghosts in there with her.

As the music unfurled, Clara searched cards and charts for signs of change. Any portent would do as long as it foretold a brighter world.

Cards whispered, casting and re-casting fate across the tabletop. Planets turned across the heavens, finding a place on each new chart only to spill away as their pencil marks were erased and drawn in again. Clara looked from Queen of Wands to Jupiter in the Second House and ignored the frail voice within her that said she alone had the power to change her lonely world.

I'm powerless.

Clara repeated this over and over, until the frail voice became silent and she no longer had to think about what it had said. Undisturbed, she let the fleeting afternoon vanish in a hunt for any sign of an external force coming to save her from the emptiness of the house. But, like every other winter's day for over a decade, the auguries offered no hope, no course to follow.

In the end, she turned off the record player knowing that it, too, was no more than a ghost.

Just once that week, Clara stood at the windows in her grandfather's study and watched Karl work. Methodically, he set out tools on the frosty patio. Breath plumed as he took down a damaged length of guttering, carefully measuring a replacement. Always, he worked with a studied pace: never rushing, never skimping.

As she watched him, Clara was struck again by the way he managed to move with the days. Always a part of the seasons, not standing outside as she did. Fingers against the cold glass, she realised she knew almost nothing about Karl despite having known him since they were both children.

Falling, her hand settled on the door handle. For a moment, she could see herself going out, speaking to Karl about… But about what, she had no idea.

She let go of the handle.

Like everything else, even something as simple as talking to Karl was beyond Clara's powers.

Spring came tentatively that year.

Winter stood back, the garden rousing itself little by little under the new season's hesitant gaze, only for spring to realise it was not yet strong enough. Hiding its face, it turned away, leaving winter no choice but to return. Patiently, the old season dressed the lengthening days in flinty taffeta and burlap gone drab with over-use. Winter held everything motionless, waiting. At last, spring returned, more confident and capable of gathering up the whole garden.

Clara watched the days change while Karl, methodical as ever, moved back and forth in front of the French windows. Digging, preparing, readying the garden for the washes of colour that quickly flowed across the flower beds.

Now and then, she saw him notice her. Straightening, Karl would touch the brim of his cap or wave. Usually, Clara quickly stepped back, her face turning as if accidentally distracted by something in the room. Afterwards, as she cautiously watched Karl go back to work, she could never decide what she felt: shame, fear, or relief.

So it came as a surprise to find herself waving back one afternoon.

The dregs of a rain shower ran haphazardly down the glass. Karl walked into view, coming from the direction of the sheds at the side of the house. His head turned slightly, noticing her as if by accident, although Clara could not shake the idea that he had looked deliberately.

Karl slowed, hand rising. Clara blinked, her own hand suddenly rising in response. Karl's expression flickered very slightly before he nodded an acknowledgement. Clara was too stunned to react. She studied his face, unsure what to read into that small change of expression.

As if something had been holding her fast until then, she suddenly found the strength to turn away. Only to turn back at once and watch a while longer.

From then on, she was driven to banish the lingering grey of winter from the inside of the house. To try, at any rate. So Clara filled the hallways and rooms she used the most with flowers; early blooms Karl selected from the garden, or hot house flowers from florists in the town. She carefully built each arrangement, then placed it strategically to tempt out memories of springs past.

When not arranging flowers, Clara took up her old water colour paints and, for the first time in years, painted sketch after sketch. Pastel washes littered her grandfather's study, hiding the Tarot deck, the knitting put aside for another year. She tried, over and over, to capture a sense of the flowers about the house; a little of their vibrancy or scent picked up by the brush to be left on the paper. Sometimes, Clara almost felt she was succeeding.

Except as mysteriously as the urge had arrived, it as swiftly left her. Only a void remained, something it seemed impossible to fill. In years past, Clara usually whiled away the spring listlessly cleaning the house; entering some long-shuttered room to move the furniture a little before abandoning the task to wander to the next room and the next. Now, not even the familiarity of this ritual held any appeal and she found herself filling the days by going back to her Tarot deck and horoscopes.

Spreads were dealt and re-dealt. Charts drafted only to be screwed up and started again. At first, Clara searched for a sign, or a hint of comfort at least. Finding neither, she carried on. Soon, all sense of purpose was gone, taking hope and any awareness of the passage of time with it. All that remained were simple physical actions and she allowed herself to be lost in turning over a card, or writing out planetary alignments.

Until, quite abruptly, even this was no longer enough.

Clara sat back. The deck of cards rested loosely in one hand, the other caught out in mid-air. With a sigh, she let that hand come to rest on the card table and turned to look around. It was almost as if her grandfather's study had just that instant come into existence. Being conscious of her surroundings again felt strange.

A newspaper lay, masthead uppermost, on an occasional table beside her elbow. It was so neatly placed it could only have been left by Karl, although she had no recollection of his having been inside the house for months.

It was dated for the last week of May. Clara stared at the newspaper, unsure what to feel. Her last certain memory was of a time towards the end of April. A month gone, the spring almost gone with it.

A glimmering pool of afternoon sunlight fell through the French windows. The halo flexed, breathing suggestions of a world beyond the room that quietly moved along without need of signs or portents. Dust drifted through the light, powerless to halt its endless fall. Clara watched the glowing motes and saw only herself: gripped by forces outside her control, unable to find peace.

It was a hateful thought. Sickening, inescapable. And there was nothing she could to about it.

'I am powerless,' she whispered. Then, before she had chance to realise what she was saying, she added, 'Because I'm afraid.'

Clara sat, even more afraid now she had admitted out loud what she had not dared face before. The words hung in the silence, refusing to fade.

Anxiously, she looked at the cards spread across the table in front of her. Cups, wands, coins, swords: all had lost their significance. Any secrets they might have held had been erased by her admission. The remaining cards slipped from her hand and sprawled across the card table. One card fluttered to the floor, the Hermit lying so the robed figure's head pointed towards Clara. Five minutes earlier, this would have been an omen. However, staring at the card, Clara felt nervous for quite a different reason.

'I want to change...' She meant it as she said it. But, could she really do it? Or would her fear—

She launched herself towards the glazed doors. Sunlight laid a comforting hand on her face. Blossoms nodded on the trees, flowers turning their heads to the sky. Partly hidden by bushes and the frame of the window, she could just see the summerhouse at the end of the garden. It had been such a special place. She still remembered it vividly when many other childhood memories had become lost in the silence clotting the house.

Now the little building was abandoned, forlorn. Like the dust, she saw something of herself in the summerhouse. She glanced back towards the card table. Fortune telling would not rekindle the magic that little building once had. Perhaps nothing could. Perhaps nothing could lift her fear either.

Not daring to reconsider, Clara tugged open the French windows and lurched out on to the small patio overlooking the garden.

The scent of fresh-mown grass mingled with the blossoms' perfume, warm air cradling her. A blackbird unfurled a rolling melody that hopped from tree to tree. Clara waited, expecting panic to force her back indoors.

Karl wheeled a barrow full of weeds and grass clippings around the side of the house. Spring was always a contented time when he could work the day round and not have to worry about having nothing to do.

He saw Clara standing beside the open doors, looking at the garden, the drifting clouds. Surprise made him pause. In his way, he had begun to turn over the idea that perhaps she would never leave the house again. Recovering quickly, he rested the wheelbarrow a respectful distance from his employer and waited for her to speak to him.

Sunshine reworked her hair, making the hints of white at her temples look like silver gilt. The light softened her appearance all round, easing some of the frown lines she normally wore like a mask. The fright that often gripped her when she was outside seemed largely absent, although uncertainty remained.

'Is this a beautiful day, Karl?' Clara asked.

Karl opened his mouth to reply, then paused. He felt himself staring at her and hurriedly looked away. There was uncertainty, yes, but something that could be cautious hope, too.

Carefully, he considered her question. He did not doubt that she was in earnest, that she wanted a proper answer.

'Yes, Miss Clara,' he replied finally, 'quite beautiful.'

Clara gave a tentative smile.

Spring ripened into summer. Flowerbeds burst into colour and every tree grew lush and green. The bees, unconcerned by the heat of the turning season, wove attentively from flower to flower, like anxious suitors presenting themselves to an unending succession of eligible ladies.

As the season drew out, so Clara spent more time out doors. It was a change that came as a surprise and not without fear. Each morning, sunlight came to her bedroom window and gently woke her to another day. If she turned away, wanting to burrow under the covers, or if she tried to hide in one of the house's many silent rooms, it simply waited patiently until she had no choice but to acknowledge its presence. Then the light gently led her outside. She went reluctantly at first, afraid to feel the happiness nudging at the edges of her mind for fear something bad should happen as a result.

Gradually, she allowed herself to believe that a disaster might not materialise after all.

Instead, she sat on the steps running down from the house to the back lawn and watched the light move. Other times, she quietly watched Karl work or simply lounged, reading under one of the trees. As the lustrous days passed, her confidence grew and she ventured beyond the house once or twice for short walks.

For all that, she could not bring herself to approach the summerhouse. The difference between her memories and reality was more than Clara could face.

As he worked, Karl watched Clara gradually find her confidence. He saw, too, her reluctance to go near the summerhouse.

One afternoon, he paused beside the dilapidated building. Childhood memories came without prompting. Memories of wandering down the garden to this secluded corner. Of the summerhouse standing amidst waves of dappled sunlight. Of its shaded interior filled with Clara's laughter.

Karl shifted awkwardly.

It's just a building, he told himself again. He thought of himself as a simple, practical person. Like his father. Karl could easily imagine what his father would say if he caught his son mooning over this battered hut.

Karl turned to go back to work. He *was* a simple, practical person. Yet, as he hesitated, he could hear Clara's laughter again, see the dappled sunlight that had once filtered through the canopy of a tree that he himself had cut down fifteen years ago.

There was no sense to it, but the summerhouse held a magic for him he could not ignore. And, from those memories of her laughter, Karl was sure Clara had felt something like that, too. Once, if not now.

Karl gazed at the summerhouse and knew he had to find a way of getting her to realise something of the building's specialness remained.

So, in those times when Clara was in the house and his duties left him free, he began renovating the summerhouse. Karl went about the task as he did everything, quietly and diligently. There was a gentleness to him at all times, none more so than as he worked on the summerhouse. Nevertheless, spiders, dead leaves and the dust of forgotten years gave way before him as he cleaned the little building. Steadily, warped boards and missing shingles were replaced and weathered paint sanded away to make way for fresh coats.

Hidden by the screen of bushes, Karl worked through the sultry dog days without noticing how they set the rest of the garden lolling. Neither did he notice that these renovations quickly came to dominate his life. Only doing the work well mattered. Several weeks went by but, to Karl, it seemed no more than a few days passed before the summerhouse was ready to use again.

Abruptly aware of the heat and a knot of anxiety in his stomach, he circled the building once, twice. The structure was sound, as good as it had been during his childhood. Yet, it still felt wrong. Karl studied the summerhouse, knuckles gently rubbing his chin. The magic was still there. His work had done nothing to lessen it, but neither had his efforts brought it to the surface as he had hoped.

Then something spoke deep within him. Karl listened and, not about to argue, set off to find different paints and finer brushes than the ones he had used so far.

One morning, as she stood looking at the piles of horoscopes and still unfinished

Tarot spread on the rickety card table, Clara was surprised to find Karl waiting at the open French windows.

'Would you come, Miss? With me, I mean.'

'Of course. What is it, Karl?'

'It's the summerhouse, Miss Clara.'

Her instinct was to refuse. Lips parted, the word 'No' forming only to remain unspoken once she saw the gentle plea in Karl's expression. Silently, he led her through the garden and around the bushes masking the old building.

Except it was old no more. The summerhouse had been transformed.

Her throat closed, speech impossible. Even without asking, she now understood Karl's absences over the last weeks. Clara shuffled, the desire to run to the rejuvenated summerhouse overwhelming. All the same, she held back.

Surely the building was now no longer hers.

Elation turned sour, the day not as warm as it had been. Clara turned to Karl. After all that he had done, he had more right to the building than she. Unspoken though it was, the need for permission was plainly written across her face. Karl's eyes widened a little, the shake of his head small but very definite as he took a step back.

The summerhouse was hers. A gift.

For a moment, a wash of emotions rooted her to the spot. Then delight carried her forwards, running five paces before stopping again. This time in wonder.

Beside the first step, a dormouse peered out at her; through vines overhead, the sharp eyes of a finch. A smiling sun-face looked down from the arch over the doorway, painted in the same vibrant yellow as the daisies on the steps. Passing under the sun-face, she found a rabbit peeking around the door post. On the roof inside, a crescent moon presented its profile whilst, around it, the zodiac circled the edges of the room. Going outside again, Clara slowly walked the circumference of the summerhouse to find a tiny fairy pirouetting under the back window, a swallow falling in a graceful dive from the eves.

She slowly returned to Karl. Tears glinted in her eyes, a smile holding her face as if it had no intention of letting go. She opened her mouth, only to find there was nothing she could say that expressed her feelings. Instead, she simply squeezed his hand, placing a butterfly-light kiss on his cheek.

'Thank you,' she managed around the lump in her throat.

Karl examined his boots, unable to meet her gaze. Even with his head down, she could see summer light reflecting in the corners of his eyes. He coughed, pretending to scratch his cheeks. The tears remained as he finally looked up.

'You're welcome, Miss Clara.' Nodding once, he returned to his work.

Weeks passed and Clara continued to find something new in the summerhouse; a cluster of periwinkles at the back of the building, the little flowers painted low so they seemed to grow out of the ground; a toad on one of the newel posts, the amphibian's face sketched into a look of contentment. She tried to catch Karl adding to the summerhouse's store of magic. Beyond a smell of fresh paint, or a tiny splash on a trouser cuff, she never did see him at work.

'Thank you, Karl,' she said each time something new appeared. Karl never replied, simply nodding and turning his head so that his smile was almost invisible. How he knew what to paint, she had no idea. But, surrounded by magical animals and flowers as she sat on the small veranda, Clara was the happiest she could ever remember being.

Summer slipped into autumn and the garden took on new colours and a different expression. The summerhouse was closed until spring's return. As never before, the little building held echoes of summers past in its roof and walls, the one just gone in particular: a robin perching nimbly on the window-ledge to feed from an outstretched hand, sunsets bringing a deep rouge to the faces of the clouds, a tender heat that smoothed away frowns and cares. Small things, but enough to prime another year.

October arrived, unpacking a series of afternoons in which each was slightly damper, slightly chillier than the last. All carried firm promises that winter would be arriving soon enough. On one afternoon in particular, Karl quietly raked up newly fallen leaves. They lay like discarded footprints on the wet grass; some brown, some golden, others a deep red. Casting out the rake, Karl pulled them all into piles so that Clara could heap them in the wheelbarrow. Once the barrow was full, she trundled the load down the garden to the bonfire-mound a little way beyond the shuttered summerhouse.

As the sun once again rested its chin on the horizon to gaze through the screen of bare-limbed trees, Karl took his father's lighter and touched a flame to the mound. Grey smoke, the ghosts of summer days now gone, corkscrewed upwards, billowing on the lazy breeze. Tendrils passed over the summerhouse roof as they drifted towards a sickle moon just beginning to come into its own.

The night deepened. Clara and Karl watched as the leaves curled with a soft rustle. Summer gave up the last of its heat until next year, when the summerhouse would be opened again.

Eventually, no more than a few embers remained, glowing in the darkness like stars fallen from the indigo sky above. KR

Bruce Barnes

The landscape from allotment 130 Heaton

She'll ask about the day; what's sown and growing,
what's been mangled by the slugs, and what birds
I saw. The view won't feature in our talk
by the sink; how I feel taller, heightened,
a gardener's sweat stinging my eyes,

but I can still see above the hedge
to Baildon Moor, sunlight shifting through
a palette of browns and greens, and on a good day
the valley unfurls, like a leaf springing
towards The Three Peaks, and Turneresque spears of light.

The river Aire, canal and Saltaire are out of sight
in the dip below; a train klaxon says that they could
still be there. Who better than Claude to paint
a pre Saltaire detail, the past as lush fantasy,
and to flourish such a garden before my eyes.

Hedge clipping on Yom Kippur

The hedge needs doing, before lank privet
fattens to a thumb thick that only the loppers
will touch, before the colours of the light-play
on Baildon Moor are lost to a monoculture
of laurel green. And I'm comfortable
with my extendables: they're light, sharp enough
to poleaxe, and with their extra reach,
they feel detached from my gloved hands—

they clip, clip, clip, unforgiving,
ignoring His command against working today.
Why should I care about the trimmings
from my father's lost faith, Judaism
will go on working its way fitfully through
the mothers; and with my steadier job
clip, clip, clipping in the hedge schools
of theology, I get to keep the cuttings—

like the privet twig with a snail underleaf.
its jazzy yellow shell shouting out
from the debris of bland green. If I were
to believe, it would be in a creator
who takes a rest when needing to,
who makes a creature to startle the eye,
and having done so, leaves the rest to chance.

Sim Seger

(with thanks to the Heritage Seed Library)

A seed, cushioned between thumb and fore finger,
finds a route through my calloused skin—its way feels
like half a tickle, (I can't put my finger on it),
but shake the packet lightly, so I am
rattled as to what it might be like

to be touched, to feel fingertips ease
me away from the earth's steady pull,
another's breath quivering my roots,
the lightest of hands at the forehead
as I am coddled, but not too much,

better to be the hardy one, starting to relax
in the wrap-around home that a dibble
might have made, waiting for the soft rain
of pins and needles, to begin again,
as the self slops into a friable earth. KR

Yvonne Baker

Birch

A silver birch and I stand side by side.
I know something about its place
in the lives of aphid and chanterelle,

the secret chemical whispers of its roots,
the way it can be planed and turned
to make a table, or a besom to sweep
the musk of the old year away.
But this is not to understand.

I stand in the slip and slide of mud.
Rain, collected in the imprints
of horse hooves and criss-cross
of bicycle tyres, holds the tree
in its dark, indifferent gaze.

I consider the birch again—
the mauve shadows on its trunk,
daubs of white where bark
peels like tissue, its scars.
Sometimes it's enough to look

at the sky through branches,
content with a promise of the canopy.
Some days it's enough to stand here.

Ghazal—Moment

Light breaks on cue in morning's first moment.
Earth, sun-glazed, created new in this moment.

The day grows old but you hadn't noticed.
Evening, a deeper blue from this moment.

Cloud rain sea—ever-changing, still the same—
the eternal dance feels true at the moment.

Let go of night and long-dead stars, day's here!
Look at all you may view—a kairos moment.

Closer than your breath, silence swaddled you.
Gently the world withdrew from this moment.

Y, stop questioning, enjoy life's unfolding.
All time's woven through a single moment. KR

Kate Gough

Gift

you are rain (in all humble
providence) cleansingly clearminded
you give of your Self (in kisses
richly sweet, like plum juice) to drink,
life dribbling (once, twice) down my chin.

meadow

the buttercups are full of butter
   sunshine & sweetness,
buzz of bee lights, settles

            drinks.

Tabletop

Sky is
licking Shore
this evening, bathed
in golden summer light,

shallow, mossy rocks simple
mouth-watering sushi
displayed on long, glassy plates,

sea gulls flecks of flying salt,
preserving the feast for all.

Land ho! KR

Contributor biographies

Yvonne Baker lives on the borders of Hampshire and Sussex and her poems often include its landscape. She writes mostly around themes of identity, the inner life and home. She's an avid reader, which provides an inspiration for writing. Yvonne has been published in print and on-line magazines. Her work has been included in *Second Light, Paper Swans, Emma Press and Poetry Space* anthologies.

Bruce Barnes writes: My poems are addressed to my allotment plot, on a sloping site facing Baildon Moor, West Yorkshire with a restricted growing season because of its exposed position. The plot has been tenanted since the 1920s and it's now 25 years since I took it on. The sequence explores my relationship with the plot, and what occurs in those fruitful states between gardening activity.

Anne Bateman: After a life of travel, Anne has finally made a home in the French Basque country, in a hinterland of heavy dews and borders, where French, Basque and Spanish identities rub shoulders. In these lush, green foothills, an outsider can slow down, observe the seasons, and write about the landscape and people getting under the skin and into the heart.

J V Birch lives on Kaurna land in Adelaide between hills and sea, with the living world informing much of her work. Her poems have been anthologised, exhibited and published in Australia, the UK, Canada and the US. She has three chapbooks with Ginninderra Press and a full-length collection, *more than here*. Visit *www.jvbirch.com* to find out more.

Uma Dinsmore Tuli's practice and teaching respects the cyclical powers of the living earth, and honours human life cycles as spiritual initiations. She is at home on the Jurassic limestone country of Stroud and for the last year has sojourned in Canada. Uma is a writer, visionary, yoga therapist, educator and radical yogini. A yoga therapist with special expertise in yoga therapy for women's health, Uma is a mother of three, and has written four books on yoga for women, including the massive *Yoni Śakti* and two books on Yoga Nidrā: *Yoga Nidrā Made Easy* (Hay House 2022) and *Nidrā Śakti, An Illustrated Encyclopaedia of Yoga Nidrā* (forthcoming). Her feature in *Kith Review* draws from seven years research for the encyclopaedia. She is co-founder of the Yoga Nidra Network a radical post-lineage grassroot organisation training yoga nidrā facilitators to make yoga nidrā freely accessible to all humans in their mother tongue. Currently, yoga nidrā in twenty-three languages is available through the Yoga Nidrā Network.

You can find Uma's books at *www.yoganidranetwork.org* and her personal website at *https://umadinsmoretuli.com/*

Clive Donovan lives in the creative atmosphere of Totnes, Devon, U.K. quite close to the river Dart. He devotes himself full-time to poetry and has published in a wide variety of magazines including *Acumen, Agenda, Fenland Poetry Journal, Neon Lit. Journal, Poetry Salzburg Review, Prole, Sentinel Lit. Quarterly* and *Stand*. His debut collection, *The Taste of Glass*, is recently published by Cinnamon Press.

Mick Evans writes: I grew up in Hertfordshire, London overspill. My paternal ancestry is Welsh, maternal English. For half my life home has been Wales' fertile Towy Valley. Garn Goch's Bronze Age settlement squats on the skyline. Over the Black Mountain, end of the

Brecon Beacons, begins the industrial past. My writing life is a struggle to reconcile contrasting histories, welling up, spilling over these hills.

Suzanna Fitzpatrick's poetry is widely published. She was shortlisted for the 2019 Bridport and Ginkgo Prizes, came second in the 2016 Café Writers and 2010 Buxton Competitions, and won the 2014 Hamish Canham Prize. Living in South London, she connects to nature through running, birdwatching and shepherding at a city farm. Her pamphlet, *Fledglings*, is published by Red Squirrel Press.

Kate Gough is a Californian writer and artist currently living in North Wales. Her practice is both flighty and deep. She is wildly in love with the world, and stokes that love with words. Kate has written and exhibited for newspapers, litmags, galleries, spoken word events, and touring exhibitions around the UK and the USA. Her work can be found in *Flash Fiction Magazine*, *Wild Roof Journal*, and *Peregrine Journal.*

Marc Harshman writes: I live in northern West Virginia near the Ohio River. There goes on here the kind of independence, self-reliance, neighbouring, and husbandry I value and which also profoundly nurtures the attentiveness necessary to being a writer. Beyond that, to paraphrase Wendell Berry, I find my 'region', in the sense it most matters, is a place where 'local life is aware of itself'. I have been published widely. Appointed in 2912, I am the seventh poet laureate of West Virginia.

Simon Jackson lives in Shanghai with his wife and two children. He plays in a jazz punk band called Hogchoker. He grew up in a tiny village in Derbyshire, feeling part of the cycle of life, and has found this transplantation disturbing but inspiring. This and the birth of his children have inspired most of his recent songs and poems.

Fiona Owen writes: I live on the west coast of Ynys Môn, the island at the very top of Wales, where I love to mooch around our rambling garden and semi-wild field. It is here that I am conscious of the turning year, with its poetry of colours and intimate dynamic of *give* and *take*. With attention, 'beholding' and journaling, I find that fragments can cohere, becoming poem.

Stephanie Percival has recently moved from her town home into a village with a fabulous Mediterranean garden. The outlook from the house makes the sky look bigger and there are continual changes to observe. Best of all is the summer house, reached by a meandering path. This is the 'Writing Room', where she writes daily whilst listening to the robin sing.

Denise Steele walks most days and in all weathers on Cathkin Braes above Glasgow. She stops a lot, consulting the trees, fields, plants, streams, birds and cityscape. Often they give her ideas for poems. Always they offer perspective. She was delighted in 2020 to have a poem shortlisted for the Wigtown Poetry Prize.

Bonnie Thurston writes: I live on six acres on the side of a hill in a little valley by a creek that runs into the Ohio River. Geographically, it is both Appalachian and Ohio River Valley. Formerly a theology professor, I have published widely as a theologian and poet.

Andrea Turner is a visual artist, singer and writer living in Moray in North-east Scotland. Her visual artwork begins by immersing herself in the landscape, returning again and again to the woods, rivers and shore so that the work is informed by deep observation and the living memory of place.. She has a degree in Fine Art from Goldsmiths College and exhibits throughout Scotland. She has performed as a singer at many jazz venues and written, produced and performed sell-out shows at the Edinburgh Festival Fringe and many other festivals. Andrea has taught singing for the past twenty years and works with individuals, groups, and organisations. She has an MLitt Creative Writing from Dundee University and has written and performed two long-form spoken word and sung performance pieces featuring specially composed instrumentals by Tom Richardson (*tomrichardson1.bandcamp.com/album/beatrice-by-the-spey*)

Andrea's website is *www.andreaturner-artandjazz.co.uk/*

Sarah Watkinson lives near Oxford and in Northumberland. She is an emeritus research fellow in Plant Sciences at Oxford University, where, throughout a career as a lecturer, she specialised in the activities of microscopic fungi that sustain forests, and rot and recycle remains. Since 2012, she has been writing and studying poetry, and realising how both poetry and science involve imagination in pursuit of understanding. Her poetry has appeared in UK anthologies and magazines including *Litmus*, *Pennine Platform* and *The Rialto*, and has been successful in several competitions. Dung Beetles Navigate by Starlight is her debut pamphlet with Cinnamon Press. Earlier published work includes three editions of a co-authored textbook, *The Fungi*, and numerous scientific papers. With Jenny Lewis she organised SciPo in 2016, an event in Oxford for Science Poetry which attracted an enthusiastic attendance.

Sally Witt, CSJ, a Sister of St. Joseph of Baden, PA, has spent most of her life in industrial neighbourhoods. She is accustomed to seeing mills and their emissions in the skyline, and looks for the goodness rooted in the people and land of these places. Currently she lives in Ambridge, PA, where she writes history and poetry.

Marjory Woodfield is a writer and teacher who lived in the Middle East, but has now returned to New Zealand. She writes about diverse experiences that have inspired and moved her: from walking through the abandoned earthquake zone in Christchurch, to the story-telling walls of an Egyptian temple; simultaneously finding both beauty and poignancy in life's varied encounters.

Patrica Helen Wooldridge has an impelling need to be outside and draws inspiration from the natural landscape, birds and the weather (especially winter). She regards walking as essential in the composition of poetry. Her publications include *Sea Poetics* (Cinnamon 2018) and *Being* (Cinnamon 2020). Her new collection *Out in the Field* won the Cinnamon Literature Award 2022.

www.poetrypf.co.uk/patriciahelenwooldridgepage.shtml

We're working on the next issue

Embodiment

Kith Review no. 2, Spring, 2023

Submission guidelines and subscription information on the website:
cinnamonpress.com/kith-review/

www.ingramcontent.com/pod-product-compliance
Lightning Source LLC
Chambersburg PA
CBHW040734100426
42734CB00045BA/3492
9781788648059